The

Natural Way to Health through Controlled Fasting

CARLSON WADE

ARC BOOKS, INC.
New York

Author of:

Helping Your Health with Enzymes
Magic Minerals: Key to Better Health

TO MY MOTHER

who restored me to the road of health
by the ancient and now-modern
rejuvenation method of controlled fasting.

This edition published by ARC BOOKS, Inc.
219 Park Avenue South, New York, N.Y. 10003
By arrangement with Parker Publishing Company, Inc.
Copyright © 1968, by Parker Publishing Company, Inc.
All Rights Reserved
Standard Book Number 668-02132-2
Printed in U.S.A.

A Doctor's Foreword

The road to good health lies in the attainment and maintenance of one's body functions at their desirable levels. This plan of health should be continued throughout the lifetime of the individual. Intemperate eating, internal toxic conditions of the body, breakdowns of body organs, even obesity itself — cannot be cured — they can only be controlled. This fact makes this book a most valuable guide for getting and keeping the best of health.

Carlson Wade demonstrates in this book that we can promote our best health with recourse to his "controlled fasting" programs; how many persons have used these programs and benefitted greatly. This book is not about fasting by starvation. Mr. Wade explains just how controlled fasting copes with practically all types of poor or undesirable health situations to confer concrete and lasting benefits that will be a revelation to readers faithfully following and applying his counsel and easy to follow programs. I am confident you will find this book will unfold an enjoyable experience for you in attaining optimal health through the application of the sound principles of controlled fasting.

There is no tyranny of oppressive discipline in this book to conflict with your normal daily routine to attain glowing and dynamic health. There could be no better advice on fasting, a time-honored system for health; no better guidelines for today's healthful living — than those contained in this book for controlled fasting.

JONATHAN FORMAN, M.D.

How This Book Can Help You Secure Better Health

The use of fasting as a natural and effective means of rebuilding the body's own dynamic healing powers has been practiced by seekers of health of every race and land upon our earth. Citations of fasting appear in the Bible, the sacred writings of Buddhism and Hinduism, as well as the Koran. In ancient days, fasting was practiced by a select few, and most likely that is one reason they achieved such heights of superior wisdom, as well as a healthy and useful long life. How to use *controlled fasting, without starving yourself,* to achieve dynamic good health for modern day living, is now available to you within the contents of this book.

We are our own worst enemies in matters of health when we neglect to rid ourselves of internal toxemia (toxic poisons) that we inadvertently allow to accumulate within our bodies. The evil effect of these accumulations is to interfere with, or sometimes actually block, the normal flow of health-promoting processes within our bodies that should continually renew our health. Basically, controlled fasting is the only natural and drugless way to help our bodies function best whereby internal toxins (dangerous poisons generated in the body) can be flushed out of the body.

This book is based on recoveries of health by many people who have cooperated with the controlled fasting programs set out in the following pages. As for myself, a health expert and also medical writer, I have experienced glorious new health through controlled fasting, having previously suffered from extremely aggravated allergies, continuous fatigue and upset stomach — as well as distressing signs of premature aging of many types. These symptoms indicated that serious internal maladjustments had developed internally which seemed to be incurable by so-called conventional methods of therapy.

My programs, developed over the years for controlled fasting, are set up in this book for specific objectives or conditions of health, and call for no drugs, no surgery, no hospitalization, no special time off from your regular routine. You can build a controlled fasting plan for prompt results right in with your daily schedule whether at work, in travel, on vacation, performing homemaker duties — or any conceivable line of activities. Moreover, the what-to-do and how-to-do-it programs need not cost you any additional expense to your normal expenditures. You might even save money in the bargain for good health!

What makes controlled fasting so special? The secret lies in an unsurpassable process that takes place in your body, a completely natural one, drugless, that literally "washes out" your insides to clear the way for your amazing self-restorative powers to recharge your whole being and activate your dynamic good health which is your birthright. Once your health has been regained in full measure, this book can then show you how you may keep healthy, develop immunity to health-wreckers, experience stimulating and favorable changes in your personality, and in general become possessed of a more commanding and radiant "presence" that can only come from your internal fountain of glowing good health.

This book is organized for your easy reference for consultation regarding a health problem, including overweight. If you faithfully follow the corresponding controlled fasting programs for a specific problem, you will also be able to enjoy better nerve-muscle coordination, healthier and more youthful complexion, better and healthier breathing through clearer bronchial and lung passages, pain-free joints, increased resistance to disease and added years and years of health-packed living. Even a short 2-day fasting plan will cleanse out an accumulation of toxic debris from your circulation system and vital organs so efficiently and effortlessly that you will promptly experience a powerful sense of rejuvenation of body and mind.

You are now in possession, with this book, of the secrets of controlled fasting and how they can all form the lasting foundation for building the structure of your superior health — your most precious possession.

CARLSON WADE

Contents

How Controlled Fasting Can Rid Your Body of Poisons

YOUTH AND HEALTH BEGIN WITH INTERNAL HOUSE-CLEANING

Millions of people are going through life in a premature aging, premature ailing condition, denying themselves the rich rewards of bountiful youth and happy health because of *internal toxemia* (poisoning). This condition may be responsible for constipation or clogged bowels, see-saw blood pressure, digestive upset and cramps, tobacco addiction, overweight and underweight, conditions of senility or poor mental vigor, clogged arteries, painful arthritis, allergies, alcoholism, raw nervous tension and many other mental and physical ailments that are shortchanging you.

Yes, *internal toxemia* may be responsible for health depletion, creating sadness, melancholy, debilitating aches, and gradual deterioration of body and mind. Your body, in its physical sense, is a machine. Like any other machine, it accumulates dirt and waste material through food residues, moisture, oxygen, air. As the years pass, these deposits grow larger and larger until they reach the stage where they cause your body's machinery to bog down, to develop aches, pains, and a host of ailments that will be described in this book, together with specific easy-to-follow, at home, natural remedies.

Internal body housecleaning is a method of controlled fasting that enables you to rejuvenate your body machinery, to restore your mind and your body to better health, to add years to your life. Controlled fasting gives your body a thorough cleansing, just as you would give any machine a good overhauling.

Yes, you regularly clean out your house or apartment, discard debris and accumulated junk. Yes, you clean out your automobile and scrape off dirt and obstructions that impair full function. Yes, you clean your clothes so that they become as good as new and just as serviceable, adding years of life to these garments.

But — did you ever stop to think about cleaning out your own body insides? Years and years of neglect may have taken their toll. If you have neglected to clean your house for many years, it becomes a refuse dump! If you have neglected to clean out the insides of your automobile motor, it becomes so clogged up it loses efficiency and may go to ruin. If you have neglected to clean your clothes, they are not only unsightly but vulnerable to rips and tears.

These items must be cleaned in order to provide excellent service. Your body's insides must also be subjected to cleaning in order to give you happy health and long life.

WHAT IS INTERNAL TOXEMIA?

The word internal is derived from the Latin word, *internus,* meaning "inward" or "inside." The word toxemia is derived from the Greek word, *Toxikon,* meaning "poison." A condition of internal toxemia may be that of poisonous substances that are inside the body and that includes all portions of the body as well as the inside of the head, or cranium, which houses the brain.

These so-called poisons are toxic waste residues that have been put inside your body by breathing in unclean air (gas fumes, duct, pollution, smoke-filled offices or factories, odors in kitchens, etc.). These leftover waste products that cling to your insides and just cannot be easily removed. These waste products are also part of foods that you eat. These waste products are meant to be removed since they can be harmful to you.

Some wastes are passed off during bowel movements; more wastes are given off through the pores of your skin during normal perspiration. But many more wastes cling to your skeletal structure, your delicate glands, your internal organs, your arteries and veins, and also flow in your bloodstream. These are not so easily passed off — *they must be removed by means of internal housecleaning and this is best accomplished via controlled fasting.*

WHAT IS CONTROLLED FASTING?

The word fast is derived from the Anglo-Saxon word, *faest,* meaning "firm" or "fixed." The practice of going without food at certain times was called *fasting,* from the Anglo-Saxon, *fasten* or to hold oneself from food. Fasting is a multi-meaning word. A dictionary defines it as "abstinence from food, partial or total, or from proscribed kinds of foods."

Controlled fasting is an ancient and oft-neglected miracle health technique that is able to help rid your body of the poisons that have accumulated over the years. It is a health technique that permits you to eat, in certain combinations, in certain quantities, so that you can give your body a chance to be internally cleansed.

YOU SHOULD BE IN BETTER HEALTH

Most people today may be deceptive when it comes to their health. Your friend, neighbor, mate or co-worker will tell you that he feels okay. You, too, may say you feel fine, but is this the whole truth? You have only yourself to fool and to blame for neglecting your clogged insides. You as well as many others may be worried, nervous, confused, short-tempered or just plain tired. You look forward to your weekends so you can spend it in bed. As the years go on, you feel less and less healthy, less and less vigorous. Something is wrong. Be fair to yourself and admit it!

Company foreman forced to retire. Young Jeff was an excellent machinist. He could take apart the most complex machine, clean out accumulated debris, put it together again and make it hum like an engineer's dream. Small wonder that he was made foreman by the time he was just 32. "Going to work hard so I'll be able to send my two boys through college," was his boast. He worked diligently, smoked cigars without letup, ate too much and too often, never gave a thought about his health. "I feel fit as a fiddle," was his boast. "Never had a sick day in may life!"

But as the years went on, his skin became sallow, he developed a smoker's cough, he complained of a feeling of fullness or being bloated, excessive stomach gas, backaches and stiff or sore shoulder. "A nice vacation ought to make me as good as new," was his self-diagnosis.

Jeff went on a vacation in the country, played cards for most of the night, ate too much and too often — and returned home and to his job feeling slightly better. But it did not take long before his muscles started to ache and his limbs became stiff.

A company physician told him that he had advance symptoms of arthritis and excessive cholesterol in his bloodstream. "You've been eating too much rich food. It's all stuck to your insides," was the doctor's terse comment.

His condition worsened so that he could scarcely move about. Jeff became nervous, short-tempered, frustrated. When well-meaning persons suggested that he clean out his insides, he just laughed at them. The fact that he believed machines could run efficiently when internally cleansed had no bearing on his own body. By the time he was 40, he was forced to retire on a small pension. His wife had to go to work. His two young sons had to shelve plans for college. Jeff, the ex-foreman, should have had a better life — if he had understood that *internal toxemia* or clogged and "dirty insides" can ruin one's working power just as it can destroy a mechanical machine.

Your life should be better than you think it can be. To improve your mind and your body you must combat *internal poisoning toxemia,* by means of controlled fasting as will be outlined to you as we progress.

Leon Patrick, M.D., noted author of *How To Eat Well And Live Longer* tells us that health is a "physiologic equilibrium (balance) between external stimulation and internal reaction which enables man's physical organs to properly perform their functions.

"Any influences that disturb this organic harmony (balance) dissipate nerve-energy, and, if not soon corrected, bring on enervation." (That means a loss of vigor or health.)

CAUSE OF TOXEMIA

Dr. Patrick points out that enervation retards elimination of body wastes which causes the internal waste products or toxins to tend to remain in the body organism. "When this condition exists, we have toxemia. *Since toxemia is the presence of an excess amount of metabolic waste, it has been designated the universal cause of all so-called diseases."*

To strike at toxemia or internal wastes, it is suggested that the body insides be cleansed by means of controlled fasting. If you neglect advance warning signs, you let your health slip through your fingers, a little at a time, until you may reach the very advanced stages of chronic illness.

ADVANCE WARNING SIGNS

Dr. Leon Patrick explains that the first organ to be affected by toxemia is the mucous membrane; the next ailments or symptoms are gastric catarrh, colds or bronchitis, virus disorders of the air passages.

Other physicians have noted that *prolonged toxemia may lead to faulty mental powers, recurring headaches, declining vision, nervous tremors, short-tempered attitude, fatigue bouts, vague muscular aches, ringing in the ears, hacking coughs, frequent colds, unusual sensitivities to dust, and failure to respond to simple medications.*

These are Nature's advance warning symptoms that clogged insides and waste residues are hampering your body machinery. When you hear a knock in your auto motor, when zig-zag lines appear on your television screen, when an annoying hum is heard on your telephone line, you lose no time in taking proper care of these "ailments." You should lose no less time in looking to the ancient remedy of controlled fasting when you feel Nature's warning signs that something may be wrong with your insides!

FASTING IS NOT STARVING

The word starve is derived from the Anglo-Saxon, *steorfan,* or "to die." A dictionary definition of starving is "to reduce to a state of extreme hunger, to deprive food." Controlled fasting consists of proper portions of certain foods at certain times. Starving is to go completely without food until life ceases. As you can see, there is quite a difference.

Dr. Patrick assures us "Proper fasting is never harmful; indeed, it is often the only procedure that will conserve nerve energy and permit Nature to rally her forces for the fight against diseases."

HOW TO TEST YOUR HEALTH RATING

As stated earlier, your life should be better. You can make it better if you are honest with yourself by admitting that many of the following conditions are felt by yourself at one time or another. Be honest because you will otherwise be fooling yourself. On a separate sheet of paper, mark down either "yes" or "no" for each of the following questions:

1. Many mornings, you feel you would like to remain in bed and go back to sleep after the alarm clock has sounded.
2. Do you go through occasional bouts of constipation that give you a feeling of being bloated and stuffed-up?
3. Do you complain of a feeling of heaviness along the region of your shoulderblades?
4. You have bent down to search for an object; after a few moments of this position, when you straighten up again, do you feel dizzy? Does it take time for the feeling to go away?
5. After reading for several hours, or watching TV for two hours, or after driving for two hours, do you complain of a headache or blurred vision?
6. You'd like to eat certain foods such as steaks, desserts, cutlets or an occasional custard or pie, but do you know that you will later have an upset stomach?
7. After you finish your dinner or main evening meal, do you have a feeling of fullness that makes it difficult for you to move around?
8. After you eat a heavy meal, do you have to lie down and "snooze it off?"

9. Time after time, you have tried to give up smoking, using everything from willpower and hypnotism to special medicines, but the urge is so strong that you must continue smoking?

10. You used to walk ten, twenty blocks or a few miles with the greatest of ease. Nowadays, do you rely upon your car or a bus or look for shortcuts because you just can't walk as much and as far as you once did?

11. Do you lose your temper and feel unable to reason things out because of a lack of patience?

12. Are you a victim of either low or high blood pressure?

13. Do you have either a slight or advanced condition of arthritis or arteriosclerosis or hardening of the arteries?

14. Do you catch a cold almost every winter? (A cold need not be so severe as to put you to bed; do you sneeze, cough, have sniffles?)

15. When you last visited your dentist, did you need to have much dental work done?

16. Take a look in the mirror. Are there circles under your eyes? Is your skin tone sallow and aging? Do you honestly (be honest, please!) admit that you're not looking as young as you *should?*

17. At times, do you have a pain in your back, lump in your throat, ache in your tummy?

18. Are you becoming addicted to alcohol? Again — be honest or your efforts will be to no avail. Must you have a cocktail or highball every single day? Is alcohol part of your life?

19. Do you have stomach aches or digestive upsets?

20. Are you lapsing into the defeatist attitude: "Oh, what's the use? I'm just getting older "?

How to score your health rating: If you have marked between 1 and 8 "yes" answers, it means that some warning symptoms should alert you to the condition of internal toxemia. If you have marked between 9 and 15 "yes" answers, it means that your insides are clogged and you should lose no time in discovering the powers of controlled fasting. If you have marked over 15 "yes" answers, you have neglected your health and should start, without delay, in cleaning out your insides.

BEGINNER'S FAST

The noted Swiss healer, Dr. Alfred Vogel, author of *The Nature*

Doctor, understands that controlled fasting for the beginner is something special. You cannot abruptly stop eating. Controlled fasting is an ancient technique that permits you to eat with pleasure and satisfaction. His suggested one-day controlled fast is sufficiently nutritious and especially designed for those who are starting out on their internal housecleaning plan.

Before Breakfast: Take half a glass of raw potato juice diluted with room temperature water. (Grate potatoes and strain out the juice.)

Breakfast: Bowl of whole wheat that has been soaked in water for two or three days. Make more palatable with a good vegetable stock. Whole grain bread with soya butter and sprinkled with wheat germ flakes. To improve bowel function, add psyllium or freshly ground linseeds to the wheat.

Luncheon: A good, strong vegeable soup with about one glass (average 8 ounces) of raw and freshly squeezed cabbage juice added, after the soup has been taken off the fire. Now a dish of steamed brown (unpolished) rice, bowl of millet, steamed seasonal vegetables that cannot be eaten raw, and a portion of raw fresh vegetables. For salad dressing, use lemon juice mixed with apple cider vinegar. If you are troubled with nervous conditions, beat a raw egg until fluffy and add to a glass of freshly squeezed grapefruit juice.

Dinner: This may be similar to your breakfast. You can vary the whole wheat dish by taking oat porridge — or put raw, soaked oats through a blender and eat with a spoon.

You may obtain the above foods at almost any produce store; visit a health food store for organically grown and spray residue-free fruits and vegetables as well as for unbleached whole wheat products.

The above controlled fasting menu permits you to eat, but is carefully composed of easily digested foods that leave little waste residue. You can fast and enjoy food at the same time!

11 BENEFITS OF CONTROLLED FASTING

Controlled fasting works to eliminate conditions of internal toxemia and thereby strengthen your body to help overcome conditions of mental and physical distress.

For example, fasting will cause a more rapid absorption of infectious fluid which has accumulated in the tissues. Or, an unnatural growth in the body may be controlled and eventually reduced or it may be completely absorbed by controlled fasting. While you are under the influence of controlled fasting, your body has a chance to readjust itself, to normalize its secretions and excretions, to bring these to a state of equilibrium. Here are 11 wonderful benefits:

1. Controlled fasting gives your entire internal organ system (heart, digestive apparatus, kidneys, lungs, pancreas, liver, etc.) a chance to rest and recuperate.
2. Controlled fasting stops the intake of foods that decompose in the intestines and further add toxic wastes to your body.
3. Controlled fasting empties your digestive tract and gets rid of putrefactive bacteria.
4. Controlled fasting enables the organs of elimination, such as your intestinal canal, to rest and become strengthened.
5. Controlled fasting helps to re-establish normal physiological chemistry and normal secretions.
6. Controlled fasting promotes the breaking down and absorption of exudates (wastes), effusions, deposits, damaged tissues and unnatural growths.
7. It will restore a youthful condition to your cells, tissues, arteries, and rejuvenate the entire system.
8. It will allow the conservation and rechanneling of energy and vigor.
9. Controlled fasting improves the powers of digestion and assimilation.
10. Controlled fasting will clear up your thinking and help build your mind power. Memory is improved. Senses are sharpened.
11. Controlled fasting will put a youthful sparkle in your eye, a bounce in your walk, a purpose in your existence.

And finally — *controlled fasting has the power to make your health better than it ever has been!* Proper abstention from certain foods in controlled fasting helps your body to eliminate (naturally) most of the excess residues lying in your stomach and intestines, also to rest up the entire digestive system so that it will later be able to handle the converting of foods more efficiently for your well-being.

Highlights of Chapter 1.

1. Your insides become clogged and debris-ridden in the course of time just as the insides of any machine, and require cleaning.
2. Most ailments are caused by an accumulation of such debris that is known as a condition of *toxemia*.
3. Fasting—more correctly—*controlled fasting* is an ancient health technique that lets you eat in regulated quantities so that you can help clean out your insides.
4. Test your own health rating with the 20-point quiz to see if Nature's warning signals are trying to tell you of your gradual health decline.
5. As a starter, try the special Beginner's Fast for alternate days of just one week.

2

Fasting Secrets of the Ancients

"As far as I'm concerned," declared Andrew J., a top salesman for a plastics company, "this business about fasting is just so much nonsense."

His wife, originally slim and attractive, had "let herself go" by eating at will and at sight until she was now a shapeless woman, looking far more than her 38 years. "I've got to try something," she insisted. "I'm just too heavy. I was told about controlled fasting that lets me eat and reduce."

"It's just another new whim," was his stubborn protest while he continued to stuff himself until he had to let notches out of his belt and buy new clothes because he was getting so corpulent. "It'll pass."

I pointed out to Lillian, his wife, that fasting was used by many people mentioned in the Bible. "It did a lot for them. Maybe it'll do the same for you both." Following is a basic controlled fasting plan:

1. Upon arising, one hour before breakfast, a glass of boiled water (sufficiently cooled, of course, before drinking) to which has been added the juice of one-half lemon and four tablespoons of apple cider vinegar.

2. On every evenly-numbered day of the month, breakfast consists of one soft boiled egg, one whole banana, coffee substitute or skimmed milk. On every odd-numbered day of the month, breakfast is a treat of diced dates, figs, raisins in a bowl or soya milk. Follow with a cup of coffee substitute or goat's milk.

3. Lunch should consist of raw vegetables in any combination followed with a glass of sauerkraut juice. (Health stores sell these in cans.)

4. Dinner, on evenly-numbered days, should be composed of vegetable broth, protein-rich meat substitute, dessert of seasonal fruit.
5. Regularly, drink freshly squeezed fruit or vegetable juices.

Just 30 days on this diet and Lillian looked better, felt better, was much younger in attitude. As for her doubting Andrew, he put on so much weight, his doctor told him to cut down on eating or run the risk of a heat attack. He had to endure privation because he was a glutton and refused to accept the ancient idea of *eating in moderation* — eating to live — and not living to eat — as a means of sustaining health.

Meat substitutes. Controlled fasting is a delicious event with meat substitutes. These are especially prepared foods made of vegetables and gluten (cohesive wheat substance) and soybeans. Most health stores sell such meat substitutes in canned form. Brand names such as Loma Linda, Emenel Foods, Worthington Foods, Lange, Elam, to name a few, are very popular. You can get foods that will taste like chicken, fish, steak, meat, scallops, liver, etc. The taste is so natural, you can hardly believe that they are made entirely from vegetable or peanut stock. Many have a nut or seed base.

These meat substitutes are invaluable for a controlled fast because they require less digestive effort, have less waste residue than most meats and some fish. If you are one who has a craving for meat, you will discover satisfaction when you use these substitutes. Nutritious and healthy, they are excellent during the controlled fast program.

REFERENCES TO FASTING IN BIBLICAL TIMES

Fasting was a known health remedy among the ancients. Moses, when he approached God on Mount Sinai to receive the Ten Commandments (Exodus 24:18, 34:28), fasted for 40 days and 40 nights.

Elijah fasted for 40 days before reaching the mount of God. (I Kings 19:8.)

David fasted for seven days during the illness of his child, breaking it at the end with bread. (II Samuel 12:20.)

Jesus fasted for 40 days and 40 nights. (Matthew 4:2.)

Luke openly stated, "I fast twice in the week." (Luke 18:12.)

"This kind goeth not out except by prayer and fasting" (Matthew 17:21.)

A fast was declared throughout all of Judea in order to obtain a greater closeness with God. (II Chronicles 20:3.)

According to the law of Moses, there is to be a one-day fast on the Day of Atonement or Yom Kippur, the Jewish New Year. No eating of any sort is permitted from sunrise to sunset.

The Bible has these tips about fasting:

1. When you fast, do not have a sad face but be clean and cheerful. (Matthew 6:16-17.)
2. Be honest, be sincere. Fast for honest and truthful purposes. (Matthew 6:18.)
3. "In the day of your fast, ye find pleasure and exact all your labors." (Isaiah 58:3.)
4. "Then shall thy light break forth as the morning, and thine health shall spring forth speedily." (After the fast, there is a feeling of lightness and health.) (Isaiah 58:8.)
5. "The fast of the fourth month and the fast of the fifth and the fast of the seventh and the fast of the tenth shall be to the house of Judah joy and gladness and cheerful." (Zechariah 8:19.) Here we see that fasts were regularly utilized and did help create a happy and cheerful disposition.

The ancients may not have known about psychiatry couches, but *they knew that troubled minds could be cured by controlled fasting!*

SEVERE FASTS

As a means of gaining worldwide attention, many idealists have resorted to "fasting". Actually, these people sought to obtain certain political or social reforms by calling attention to their self-denial — and then labelled it fasting. In reality, these idealists *starved* themselves because they *abstained completely from all forms of food.*

Mahatma Gandhi, who was assassinated at 84, fasted frequently and often for as long as 50 days. He refused all food except some water. Many others went on hunger strikes in protest over certain political rulerships. Unhappily, their hunger strikes or starvation sieges were termed "fasts" by the newspapers, and today *most people associate fasts with complete deprivation of food. Nothing could be more wrong!*

CORRECT FASTS

Two great philosopher-teachers, Socrates and Plato, would fast before undergoing severe mental stress during which they would write on philosophy. They would abstain from foods for 10 days at a time.

Pythagoras, another Greek philosopher, fasted for 40 days before takeng a special test at the University of Alexandria. He required that his pupils do the same, believing that proper fasting would stimulate physical and mental powers.

These were correct fasts because they were conducted for purposeful gains. However, you are not to deny yourself food for such long periods. The point is that these ancients ate very sparsely for most of their lives. Their digestive systems were tamed and could endure prolonged fasting. After a lifetime of heavy meat, eggs, fish and otherwise protein-carbohydrate-caloric eating, you are not expected to shock your nervous system by abrupt withdrawal of foods. But you can gradually reduce and eliminate portions, heavier foods and adjust to controlled fasting.

SIMPLE FAST PLAN

J. DeWitt Fox, M.D., in *Life And Health* (Vol. LXXX, No. 1) suggests a simple fast plan whereby you do the following:
1. Cut out meat.
2. Eliminate all highly seasoned gravy.
3. Eliminate rich cake and sugary preserves.

"Such a fast proves of more benefit than medicine, for the abused stomach finds the rest it has long needed."

YOU CAN EAT WHILE YOU FAST

Is this possible? Yes, with controlled fasting, you can ease your hunger. Take a tip from the desert Bedouins of North Africa. For days on end, they survive quite hardily on a diet consisting of dates, raisins and goat's milk. They chew these natural foods (not the milk, of course) and predigest them and wash down with goat's milk. The natural grape sugar in the dates and raisins provides much energy. The storehouse of vitamins, minerals, proteins, enzymes, in goat's milk provides precious nutrients. Obtain sun-dried dates and raisins at health stores, along with canned goat's milk, or powdered goat's milk that you mix with water.

7 REWARDS OF CONTROLLED FASTING

"What's in it for me?" asks a housewife and mother of 4 children who is always tired, losing her looks, getting a paunchy and unlovely appearance. "What will controlled fasting do for me? Am I selfish in so asking?"

No, indeed not. It's your body — and you want to treat it properly. You have every right to know how controlled fasting will improve your overall health. According to Dr. J. DeWitt Fox, here are 7 rewards made possible when internal toxins have been cleaned out from your mind and body:

1. *Well-being.* "The general well-being of a person on a fast has been noted by physicians," says Dr. Fox. "Many a doctor advises fasting for a patient tussling with gout, heart disease, skin disorder, general intemperance to food and drink, or excessive smoking."

2. *Cleansing tonic.* The doctor says that the speediest way to "rid the body of certain toxins and impurities or to overcome a cold or the flu is to fast and drink copious amounts of water." A periodic fast helps prevent illness. The practice of controlled fasting "serves as a cleansing tonic to the body if large quantities of water are taken and good elimination is established before and during the fast."

3. *Super brain power.* Fasting benefits your brain; it sharpens your mind, makes you alert and sensitive to mental effort. *How?* Your powers of concentration are increased if your stomach is empty and not drawing blood away from your brain to digest food. Many a public speaker knows that eating before speaking will reduce mental acuity and reduce speech power. Here is their general rule — *"Fast before an important speech and eat later."* A big

company president told me that he schedules all board of directors meetings at 10:30 A.M. "Our minds are sharper because we've had breakfast about two hours before and lunch is about two hours away."

4. *Relieve digestive upset.* Your stomach, liver, pancreas, and intestines are frequently much overworked. Give your digestion machinery a vacation. As Dr. Fox points out, if you drink plenty of water while fasting, there is practically no danger of your developing a dangerous ulcer, or other stomach malady. In fact, many cases of colitis and intestinal disorder are greatly benefited by a periodic fast. which puts the intestines at rest. If you take nothing but water and use no sweet drinks or starches, your pancreas also is placed at rest, and which also reduces hunger pangs. When hunger disappears, insulin is not required to work out the glucose in your bloodstream. Glucose is produced by large amounts of starchy and sweet foods.

5. *Rejuvenate, refresh your skin.* Those who fast, note many physicians, acquire a much clearer skin, a rosier tint to the cheek. Acne, psoriasis, recurrent skin infection may be relieved and better controlled by eliminating all sweets and all fats from the diet. How much better it is to eliminate all foods for a time periodically, and let the skin pores have a chance to cleanse themselves and be free from the clogging effects of too many sweets and fats.

6. *Helps stop smoking, drinking urge.* Toxic wastes have a chance to be dispelled while you fast and this eases the urge or craving for smoking and drinking which, by the way, are traced to nervous disorders. Nerves are involved in food digestion, too. Excessive eating causes excessive nervous response or reactions. That's why many folks reach for a smoke or a drink after eating. Overworked nerves "scream" for these drug-like substances. Warm baths in moderation help you eliminate noxious products left in your body by smoking and drinking into the water. After you "scrub clean" your insides by fasting, you feel more alert, more alive, and less of an urge to reach for a drug-like stimulant such as tobacco, alcohol etc.

7. *Gives your heart a rest.* Digestion is made possible by a copious flow of blood; your heart pumps to send a supply of blood to the digestive system. A fast obviously then takes a load off your heart and your circulatory system. If you have been short of breath, a fast will improve your breath-power; fasting will eliminate salt and

water from your body, reduce tissue edema (swellings), relax your heart and give you a feeling of welcomed peace and contentment. After all, who can deny that a happy heart is a healthy heart — and vice-versa?

WHY THE DOCTOR FELT PEPPIER

"Not long ago," relates Dr. Fox,

I tried a 5-day fast (for weight reduction, of course). The most impressive finding was lack of fatigue and freedom from hunger after 48 hours. I actually felt sharper mentally, and was able to perform heavy surgical operations with skill and mental alertness equal to what I had when eating. A feeling of euphoria (buoyant health) is noted by some people on a fast, and this was my experience. I actually felt peppier and more alert mentally. I slept more soundly than when eating regularly!

EAT WELL WHILE YOU FAST

This sounds like double-talk, but it's actually true! You *can* eat while you fast. The secret here is that you eat lighter foods, those that have valuable nutrients but require less digestive power and leave less toxic wastes as are left by meats, fish, poultry, etc.

The ancients knew of this secret and that is undoubtedly the reason for their survival even on prolonged fasts. They would devote eating attentions to fruits and vegetables. The beginner on a fast would do good to alternate — one day to reduce intake of your normal foods. The next day — you eat fresh vegetables in salad form, drink freshly squeezed vegetable juices. The third day — back to your reduced intake of normal foods. The fourth day — turn to fresh fruits in salad form and freshly squeezed vegetable juices. The fifth day — to your reduced intake of normal foods. The sixth day — your vegetable fare.

Occasionally, have two days of vegetable eating and fruit eating. That is, a vegetable day follows a fruit day, then you follow with reduced intake of normal foods.

There you have the very synthesis of *controlled fasting* — you can eat your cake (in a manner of speaking) and have it, too! (A sound nutritional program should *avoid cake* because of the bleached, artificial substances that leave a quantity of ash residue in the system, adding to the over-burdened toxic condition.)

THE BASIC TECHNIQUES OF CONTROLLED FASTING

This ancient method of internal cleansing is beneficial when managed in the use of these techniques:

1. *Elimination.* Certain offending foods that leave harmful toxic wastes in the system — that accumulate until a condition of toxemia arises to slowly decrease health — should be eliminated from your diet. This calls a halt to the adding of harmful substances. Fasting methods (described later on) enable your body to cleanse itself of the accumulation of toxic wastes.

2. *Reduction.* Some foods are necessary to your health but because of residual content left in your body should be eaten in moderation. Reduce your intake of sugar-containing foods if you are gaining weight, for example. Reduce carbohydrate-containing foods if your skin has unsightly blemishes. Reduce acid-containing foods if you have a perspiration problem. Chapters following in this book will suggest specific food-reduction fasting schedules for individual problems.

3. *Substitution.* Controlled fasting is a marvelous technique that lets you *enjoy your favorite foods* while you undergo internal cleansing. This is done by the method of substitution — if you love chocolate but have unsightly blemishes and gaining unhealthy pounds, you substitute these sweets with those that are chocolate-free but contain *carob,* a *chocolate tasting* seed-derived powder that is delicious and non-toxic. If you must reduce intake of fats, look to vegetable oils and vegetable-derived fats such as sunflower seed oil, safflower oil, corn oil. Controlled fasting works perfectly with substitution.

4. *Combination.* Proper food combination is most essential in keeping clean and healthy insides. For example, starch and protein foods, eaten together, form a troublesome "glue" that leaves gummy wastes adhering to your digestive tract. Eat these types of foods *separately.* Later chapters will show you how you can eat certain so-called offending foods. singly or in *special combination,* or in a certain schedule, and thereby reduce chances of clogging up your insides with unhealthy, ashy residues.

Throughout it all — controlled fasting lets you eat while you clean out your insides and open the way to vibrant health. The ancients well knew the secrets of natural health; the fasting secrets will now be passed along to you as they have stood the test of time from antiquity.

In Review:

1. Because protein foods digest into amino acids and leave some residue, try delicious meatless substitutes which have more easily assimilated amino acids. Available at most health food stores.
2. Bible personalities and ancients often resorted to controlled fasting.
3. Bedouins would fast upon a diet of dates, raisins and goat's milk. Try it, yourself, for one day. It's a wonderful "quickie" internal cleaning program and will be a revealing good health experience for you.
4. You have 7 rewards for controlled fasting, ranging from physical well-being to super brain power.
5. There are four basic techniques to follow when undergoing a controlled fast — food elimination; food reduction; food substitution; and food combination.

3

How Anyone Can Fast
Efficiently and Easily

When controlled fasting is built into your schedule, it is surprisingly easy to follow this health-rejuvenation plan. It is a technique that can be utilized while you are on your job, or on a vacation, *and even during weekends.* It is possible for housewives to enjoy controlled fasting with as much simplicity as the working girl, or for the blue and white collar worker and the professional man. Here are some tips.

HOUSEWIFE'S FAST

Susan is the mother of three youngsters and the wife of an insurance salesman. "Want to know how I can fast while my hungry brood continue eating?" She had developed this plan. She awakens an hour before the rest of the family. Before she starts breakfast for them, she eats two fresh apples or two pears or any natural fruit, (she dislikes canned fruits that are packed in heavy syrups), and follows this with two glasses of freshly drawn tap water. The minerals in the fruit become "supercharged" when followed with fresh water. The resultant action works upon the internal toxins and waste substances that have remained from days before. The minerals attack these substances, devour and otherwise help destroy much ash residue, cleansing her insides.

"Sure, I eat breakfast with my family, but prefer lighter foods than their corn flakes (the starch granules adhere to the digestive tract) or French toast (the bran content also leaves behind toxic wastes that have accumulation tendencies). I prefer a bowl of freshly sliced fruit with yogurt. It lasts me until noon time and I then eat a vegetable salad with cottage cheese and drink a glass or two of freshly squeezed vegetable juice or a cup of piping hot herb tea."

You can get a variety of exotic herb teas at any health store; most gourmet shoppes sell them, too.

At the main meal, Susan eats lean meats with all visible fats removed, completely avoids salt because the reaction may whip up whatever internal toxins remain into a frenzy that may erupt into skin lesions, sniffles, allergic reactions, bloodshot eyes, etc.

"I hope I can use myself as a good health example for my husband so he'll be able to improve himself with controlled fasting as time goes on. The children are next on my schedule."

THE WORKINGMAN'S FAST

If your company has a cafeteria, learn to select those foods which are least likely to cause accumulation of internal debris. Later chapters of this volume give offending food lists for specific conditions. If your co-workers turn up their noses at your peculiar eating habits, explain that you are on a special diet and that's that.

WEEK-END FAST

If you can get away from it all for a 3-day weekend, you can reap wonderful benefits from a stepped-up fasting plan. Here's how:

First Day — Reduce quantities of all your meals; the third or evening meal should consist exclusively of raw vegetables and freshly squeezed vegetable juices or a glass of canned vegetable juice such as sold by health stores. You can buy a few cans and take them along with you on your vacation weekend or in your home, depending upon where the fasting plan is being conducted.

Second Day — Your three meals should consist exclusively of raw fruits and raw vegetables and juices made from these foods. To satisfy that desire to chew, try chewing succulent fruits such as apples, pears, peaches, or juicy vegetables such as lettuce, tomatoes, celery.

Third Day — Raw fruits and baked vegetables — try baked potatoes, eggplant, beets and squash and meatless substitutes. This is a wonderful and invigorating internal housecleaning plan for a weekend fast program.

ON-VACATION FAST

An office girl I know selects resorts that permit cooking and brings along a supply of fresh fruits and vegetables. She lives on a controlled fasting program during her vacation, alternating between cooked vegetables and raw vegetables. All her fruits are eaten raw. When she comes back to the office, she looks as radiant as if she had been to a health resort. In a way, she has! Vacation is a good time to start fasting and initiate yourself into this program since you're in a relaxing, tension-free environment.

WORKING GIRL'S FAST

Want to avoid constant cold-catching? Want to have a clearer skin, shinier hair? Want to keep a trim figure? To follow the controlled fasting techniques suggested in later chapters, you may bring your lunch to your office and thereby simplify the problem of selected foods. If you eat out, look for a health food store in your vicinity that serves natural foods. Or find a restaurant or cafeteria that will provide you with your desired foods.

Once you get into the plan, it will be comparatively easy to follow the technique of controlled fasting.

REJUVENATE YOURSELF

By means of controlled fasting, you can easily rejuvenate yourself. Robert G. Jackson, M.D., author of *How To Be Always Well*, tells us,

> Fasting is a most wonderful process of rejuvenation. *Aging is the result of accumulation of poisons in the body.* Disease is, in my view, due to the same cause, primarily, at least. The body that has no struggle with fatigue poisons, or tissue and food debris, because the eliminative processes have been kept normal

by natural means and have not been imposed upon by unnatural living habits, will find every cell and organ functioning normally. When this is the case, the body must be absolutely perfect, and a perfect body must be free from disease. Such a body can laugh at microbes.

CONTROLLED FASTING AND COLDS

Dr. Jackson suggests going on a fruit fast at the first signs of a cold — your diet should consist solely of fruits in natural form such as a salad, or in juice form. Abstain from all other foods for a period of two days — but drink as many freshly squeezed juices as you want and eat a wide variety of seasonal fruits (uncooked) throughout this two day period. The result? You will undergo internal housecleaning and ease cold symptons.

Says the doctor, "It is a well known fact that, although the poorly-fed body is apt to 'catch cold' and suffer from various catarrhal and inflammatory affections of the respiratory tract mucous membranes, *a fasting person never 'catches' cold*.

"On the other hand, colds and catarrhal and inflammatory affections rapidly clear up during a fruit fast."

HOW COLDS ARE CAUSED BY TOXEMIA

Dr. Jackson, quite firmly, states that colds are a "reaction by which the body seeks to rid its debris-burdened cells of their encumbering substances via the mucous membranes. I stated that this debris is always deposited in the tissues because it is so in excess in the bloodstream that it cannot be all carried in solution or suspension."

When you have a cold and continue eating regular foods, the blood "will not reabsorb any of the substances formerly dropped by the wayside in the tissues and body cells."

HOW FASTING MAY RELIEVE COLDS

When you go on a fruit diet and drink water freely, your blood soon becomes "hydremic" or watery and, according to a medical authority, the blood's specific gravity and density-only materials available through digestion are those foreign substances formerly dropped by the wayside among the tissue cells. These substances are redissolved in the blood and taken back into circulation. They are then burned up or oxidized and eliminated, generally as water and gas, by the skin and mucous membranes.

Thus, your body "cleans house" during a fast. Frequently great quantities of mucous will be eliminated by the lung system during a fast, but the nagging and inflamed evidences of a cold are almost always absent. When these symptoms are present, they are indicating a systemic encumbrance or stoppage that the body must be rid of if its is to become well and resist disease. And the one sure way to rid the body of accumulated poisons (internal toxemia) is to keep fasting until these mucous elements are ejected from your system.

Whether you are a housewife, working man or woman, travelling salesperson, teacher, student, you can enjoy controlled fasting by restricting your edibles to fresh and raw fruits and juices at the first onset of a cold and thereby enable your bloodstream to become hydremic so that it will be able to clutch at toxic wastes — those same toxic wastes that may be responsible for your virus infection — and redissolve them, burn them up and eliminate them.

HOW TO BE IMMUNE TO COLDS

Immunity to colds can be cultivated by eating fruit in goodly amount. The acid content of fruits are the best tissue alkalinizers and internal systemic cleansers known.

Eating simple meals of fruit, and thereby eliminating troublesome accumulations within the body, is health step No. 1. In all forms of sickness, even colds and depressions of every kind, one can live without tremors in his muscles and nerves, and in the pink of physical fitness always.

HOW FASTING WORKS IN YOUR BODY

In a word, the secret and active ingredient of fasting is *autolysis*. The word is taken from the Greek; it means "self-loosing." Physiologically, it designates the process of disintegration of "sick" tissue by enzymes generated in the cells. Autolysis is a process of self-digestion and absorption.

During any condition of health deficiency, whether it be a cold, cough, acne or stomach upset, there is an accumulation of internal toxic and poisonous substances. These are masses of diseased particles that conspire together to cause an ailment. How do you get rid of this internal debris? (You doubters can see toxemia in the form of a pus pimple, or abscess, on the surface of your skin. This little pocket of infection is composed of dead wastes and accumulated debris that your body wants to expell by any means, including puncturing the skin.)

You may insist, "My body can get rid of these wastes somehow without fasting."

To a certain extent, this is true as we see by bowel movements, perspirations, coughs, blinking of eyes when foreign matter enters, etc. But there are limits. Without controlled fasting, *autolysis* cannot completely function to destroy the dangerous accumulations of waste materials.

On the one hand you have millions upon millions of enzymes or digestants in your system. These enzymes look for foods to attack and break down into usable nutrients, and then discard the rest. On the other hand, when you introduce copious amounts of foods to keep your enzymes busy (often, overworked), they have no time or strength to attack these waste substances.

When you fast correctly, you force your enzymes to look for other things to work upon. Seeing any accumulation of cells such as a pimple, cyst, abscess, etc., they attack these substances. The enzymes then digest these internal accumulations and cause them to be excreted through your skin pores. Without enzyme action, these internal accumulations cling to your delicate body organs, glands, bloodstream, arteries, set up an unhealthy condition that predisposes you to sickness.

Before this *autolysis* or "self-loosing" process can be released upon your internal wastes, you must deprive your enzymes of food so they will then be forced to attack these waste materials.

In this way, your enzymes will be forced to become cannibals and devour these infectious accumulations when they are denied food during a fast! They just have to keep busy, and will not lie dormant.

How quickly can autolysis work? Give yourself a one-day fast and your enzymes start the autolyzing process. For the full story of enzymes, read my book, *Helping Your Health and Enzymes*[1], a comprehensive self-help work devoted exclusively to this subject. You will be glad that you did!

FASTING AND BODY GROWTHS

By means of controlled fasting, many people have gotten rid of body growths — blood, flesh and even bone growths. Tumors are tissue-composed, and many are susceptible to autolytic disintegration. During a controlled fast, such tissues do undergo a process of dissolution and absorption. Fasting also helps reduce body fat, muscle size, and bumps caused by wads of dead tissue.

During a controlled fasting program, the accumulations of superfluous body tissues are "overhauled" and used up by enzymes and then discarded through normal channels of elimination from the body.

Bernard Macfadden, the pioneering health enthusiast, is reported to have said,

> My experience of fasting has shown me beyond all possible doubt that a foreign growth of practically any kind can be absorbed into the body's circulation by simply compelling the body to use every unnecessary element contained within it for food. When a foreign growth has become hardened, sometimes one long fast will not accomplish the result, but where they (growths) are soft, the fast will usually cause them to be absorbed.

OVER-ALL HEALTH IMPROVEMENT

Controlled fasting is a natural method of freeing your body from diseased tissues, excess accumulations of toxins and wastes. This method helps to purify your bloodstream. It expels pent-up excretions. It provides rest and relaxation to your nervous system

---

[1] Carlson Wade, *Helping Your Health with Enzymes* (West Nyack, New York: Parker Publishing Company, Inc., 1966).

and delicate organs. When you cleanse your tissues and cells and fluids, and when you wash out those accumulated internal toxic wastes, you experience a veritable re-birth and overall body improvement.

Fasting forces the body to rely upon its internal substances, forces the disintegration (by means of autolysis) of growths, accumulations, infiltrations, sweeping through your body and washing it clean and healthy.

The famed J. H. Kellogg, M.D., noted author of *New Dietetics* discovered that among his controlled fasting patients, these improvements were noted:

1. Surplus body fat was disposed of.
2. Accumulation of surplus or "floating nitrogen" or waste substances that were hitherto present and giving trouble, rapidly disappeared during a controlled fast.
3. Fasting helped create a normal and healthy appetite, ended the compulsion to overeat and to stuff one's self.
4. Fasting helped produce rejuvenation in some of the tissues.
5. After a period of controlled fasting, the patient displayed an unusual degree of vigor and an enriched and elevated sense of well-being. Controlled fasting also built resistance to infections.

BLUEPRINT FOR FASTING

Before and during your controlled fasting plan, follow these essential steps:

1. *Fast without interference.* A bookkeeper lamented, "The trouble with fasting is, there's no place to do it in." How right! Surroundings and environment are important. Family, relatives, neighbors, co-workers may conspire against you, tempt you to continue stuffing yourself or to continue eating foods not in your best interests. This could make you throw in the sponge! Of course, home is an ideal place but if you are going to be faced with ridicule and taunts, better wait until you go on a vacation — or else just put your foot down, build resistance to temptations, etc., and follow your fasting plans. In extreme situations, try to avoid coming home during mealtimes.
2. *Conserve your energy.* Controlled fasting brings about a temporarily low degree of metabolic activity so learn to save your

energy. Avoid useless physical activities. Even reading, writing, talking, listening to a noisy radio or watching an exciting TV show can burn up energy stores. Surround yourself with restful influences.

3. *Fresh air*. Oxygenate your system with much fresh air. Your living quarters should be well-ventilated. Your working area should also have a source of fresh air. During your "break" or rest period at your job, try to get out of the building and breathe in fresh air — avoid regions that have auto fumes or pollution.

4. *Keep warm*. Your hands and your feet should be kept warm during controlled fasting. Chilling causes discomfort, insomnia, nervous tension. Wear warm socks. I prefer those made with lamb's wool because of superior warming quality. These are available at most any men's store or department store.

5. *Exercise in moderation*. While you should conserve your energy, it does not mean that you just lie down throughout your controlled fasting program. Try a brisk 15-minute walk. Do setting-up exercises. Deep knee bends are helpful in moderation. A healthy body thrives on movement and this is true during your fasting program.

6. *Bathe yourself intelligently*. During controlled fasting, be careful to avoid extremes of temperature as this may shock your nervous system. Wash your body quickly. Do not remain too long in the tub or under the shower. A sponge bath is often helpful. Too hot or too cold water may prove enervating and drain your energy. Bath water should be about 98°F., or close to your own body temperature. Washing yourself thoroughly is essential to slough off waste substances that have been secreted in skin pores.

7. *Bad mouth taste*. The little papillae or nodules that occur on the tongue surface may have a bad taste during fasting. It's a good sign since the process of autolysis is excreting noxious substances through the porous surface of your tongue. To alleviate a bad taste, scrub tongue with a toothbrush and your dentifrice. As the fast progresses, the taste is less offensive; at the end of the fast, your mouth should taste naturally fresh and clean.

8. *Water drinking*. Water helps eliminate body toxins, so drink regularly. Water drinking flushes accumulated impurities out of the whole system and washes the insides. Water drinking expedites the washing out of excessive chloride of sodium, urea, phosphates and disintegrated toxemia-ridden tissues. Cold or iced water is unwise and taboo to the controlled faster because it causes a drop

in body temperature, constricting the internal organs. Drink fresh tap water or bottled distilled water that is not too chilled.

9. *When to fast?* In brief — *when it is needed!* That is, when you have certain conditions that should be cleared up. When you want better health and a better life. *No condition of impaired health should be tolerated or allowed to become more serious. Now* is the time to start restoring and improving your health; not next week, next month, or next year.

THE POWER OF CONTROLLED FASTING

There is beneficial power in the *technique* of controlled fasting. Understand that fasting allows a marked increase in the elimination of toxins and waste from your body — not only from your body fluids, but also from your body tissues. It helps your elimination organs to bring their work up to date — to balance their books, so to speak.

How does it work? When putrefactive and fermentative toxins are pouring in from your digestive tract in excess of your body's ability to neutralize and eliminate them and the toxic overflow has been partly stored in the less vital tissues, controlled fasting hurriedly stops the intake of decomposition-toxins and gives the organism a chance to catch up with its work of excretions. Controlled fasting helps remove the toxins in the tissues, causes the body to consume its excess of fat, enables the body to break down growths by means of autolysis.

Controlled fasting stops the doing of damage to the body. That's right, it calls a halt to certain unhealthy activities, withholds raw materials, stops the inflow of decomposition-poisons from the alvine canal (the abdomen or lower intestine region), facilitates the repair and recuperation of body organs, the removal of circulating and deposited toxins, the normalization of blood chemistry, cellular and tissue rejuvenation, the absorption of deposits, exudates, effusions and growths, improves body power of digestion and assimilation.

In this manner, dropsical swellings, edematous swellings, and deposits are absorbed and the usable portions salvaged for use in nourishing the vital tissues. Controlled fasting creates an internal nitrogen hunger and an internal demand for nutritive elements; this prompts autolysis or self-absorption and the internal disintegration of those offending substances undermining your health.

Controlled fasting will cause a more rapid absorption of dropsical fluid which has accumulated in the tissues than any other known measure. A skin lesion (sore) may cease growing, its size eventually reduced or possibly completely absorbed during the fast.

This ancient technique helps your body readjust itself, normalize its secretions and excretions — bring you to a state of internal equilibrium. Controlled fasting is *Nature's secret* of ridding the body of "diseased" tissues and accumulations of waste and toxins. These accumulations of surplus tissues are "overhauled" and analyzed; available component parts are turned over to the nutritive system while the harmful refuse is thoroughly removed. When these internal toxic wastes are removed, the nervous system becomes strengthened and its sensibilities become more acute. After all, as the ancients would say: "A full stomach does not like to think."

HOW YOU CAN "SEE" TOXEMIA

A middle-aged schoolteacher believed only what she could see. Edith was a realist and should be respected for her attitude. "And I saw my grandmother and my mother and my older sister develop gall bladder trouble and be operated for removal of stones. I've heard them say that gall bladder difficulties are ofter hereditary, and happen if you are female, fat and 40 — and I'm something of all three." She could not believe that gallstones are accumulations of waste substances and underwent a serious operation. Complications later developed and she became a semi-invalid. She did have gallstones, no doubt about that, but she refused to believe that fasting might have helped her condition. She could not see these accumulations!

You, too, may doubt the seriousness of these internal toxic wastes. Okay, let's show you toxemia. That's right. You can *see* internal toxemia, to a certain extent. Here's a quick run-down:

Acne. Caused by accumulations of pus and dead excreta that erupt in the shape of a fistule on any part of the body. Usually, offending substances in chocolate, spiced foods, sugar are to blame.

Dandruff. Clumps of scale tissue and slough debris given off by the sebaceous and sweat glands. Often traced to intake of starch and salt-containing foods.

Bloodshot eyes. The tiny capillaries that run like networks through the retina and pupil of the eyes become laden with accumulated debris through various sources. Smoke and grime as well as acid-containing perspiration which is heavy in waste materials that get into the eyes may cause this condition.

Fever. You can feel a fever, that's for certain. It is Nature's signal that your body is filled with microbes or toxic substances. Your body rushes white blood cells to the site of these toxic poisons, seeks to remove the debris. This causes a speed-up of the metabolism process, hence the hot feeling. According to W. G. MacCallum, M.D., in *Textbook of Pathology,* "Fever is a reaction elaborated, to a considerable degree of perfection, which aids in the defense of the body against the advance of an injurious agent by facilitating the production of the substances which are formed in the body to neutralize poisons or kill bacteria." Once again, we see that toxemia has caused this internal revolution!

Perspiration or sweating is another attempt by Nature to rid your system of some of the accumulated waste substances.

Cholesterol — ordinarily unseen, fatlike substance that clings to the arterial structure, giving rise to conditions of hypertension, heart irregularity, arteriosclerosis, etc. High animal fat intake is mainly responsible for leaving these toxic wax-like substances in the blood circulation system.

Gallstones — outwardly unseen, *biliary calculi* are concretions or crystalling of internal toxic substances that originally appeared in your bile, but have backed up and accumulated in the gall bladder. These poisonous wastes cling together in small particles and may be as tiny as a sand grain or as large as a goose egg.

Warts. These can be seen; they are caused by accumulated wastes that become lodged in the tissues of the foot or hand. To houseclean these toxic substances, here's a suggestion by Dr. Alice Chase, osteopathic physician author of *Your Health Problems:*

"Take soda baths to neutralize over-acidity of the skin secretions. A cup of baking soda or a half teacupful washing soda would be a good addition to one or two daily baths. Soap may also be used in a tub like this." Epsom salt is beneficial because of its medicinal properties, easing the nerve pain of the wart.

Because warts are unwanted parasitic conglomerations of diseased cells, the process of autolysis should be utilized. The diet should be free from sugar and starch and temporarily low on protein to permit internal self-digestion of these waste substances. Bed rest is helpful since you keep off your feet if the warts are therein situated. Increase intake of fresh raw fruits and vegetables.

Lower limb inflammation. Often know as *phlebitis,* this is an inflammation of the veins of a lower limb that may be caused when some of the waste or toxic poisons from the colon (the large bowel or intestine) become absorbed into the blood and clog the veins that extend to the leg. Fasting enables the red and white cells of the blood to turn scavenger, and devour these toxic substances so that the bloodstream becomes purified and inflammation is reduced and finally eliminated.

Puffed eyelids. Often, you see people on television or in newspapers with puffed eyelids. Nature throws fluid wastes and internal poisons into accessible pockets. The eyelids are vulnerable recipients of a small amount of cellular lymph wastes and other by-products of degeneration of the body. There are other areas of retention of these toxic substances which you can see: large abdomens that feel puffed, swollen legs and swollen ankles. Many doctors feel that meat, bread, potatoes and sugar-containing foods introduce internal substances that accumulate — especially if these foods are eaten in excess. To wash out these waste accumulations, drink freely of liquids made from fruits and vegetables. This helps improve circulation of blood and lymph in the blood vessels and drain away the store of these toxic wastes from the eyelids.

Kidney stones. Small deposits of toxic substances cling together and accumulate to form stones sometimes of large size. Pepper and alcohol are serious kidney irritants. Salt is harmful by virtue of its irritation, too. Particles of ash residue left by pepper, alcohol and salt may form into these stones. Again we see the value of controlled fasting to wash out these wastes. Eliminate eating foods containing condiments of any sort! They can help build stones to undermine your health.

Tooth and mouth disorders. Tartaric acid and harmful deposits of sugars and starches, mouth acids (the result of fermentation of carbohydrates — sugar and starches) lead to mouth disorders and tooth trouble, You can often see these unsightly toxemia deposits on tooth enamel surfaces. You can feel them by running your tongue tip over your teeth. Brushing helps. So does rinsing. Elimination of refined sugar and starch foods is by far a much greater help. To houseclean your mouth, eat whole, fresh apples. Pectin minerals, as well as Vitamins A and C, will work on these toxic waste substances and help slough them off ... and clean your tongue, too.

Succeeding chapters of this volume will be devoted to specific conditions traced to improper eating and explain how controlled fasting can help to relieve and even eliminate many diseases and disease-symptoms.

Essentials of Chapter 3

1. A housewife, a working man, a working girl can fast under certain easy-to-follow conditions.
2. Are you a chronic cold-catcher? Fasting can be your long-awaited cure, as its was for Robert G. Jackson, M.D. A fruit plan helps create hydremia which, in turn, dissolves those cold germs.
3. Autolysis or self-digestion is the secret "ingredient" of the ancient technique of controlled fasting.
4. Follow the 9-step blueprint to benefit the most from controlled fasting.
5. You can see toxic wastes manifested on the body, and you can feel them, too. A quick run-down is listed on common ailments traced to a debris-clogged system.

How to End Intestinal Trouble with Controlled Fasting

For good reason, intestinal trouble, or constipation, is regarded the source of many physical, and even mental ailments. It is usually the first faulty body condition brought about by the clutter of internal degris and internal toxic substances. Just how does this happen?

INTERNAL TOXEMIA AND CONSTIPATION

Food that you eat is first digested in your stomach, then in your small intestines. Here, the food is transformed into a smooth liquid known as chyme. The digestible portion of chyme is absorbed through the walls of your small intestines, into your lymphatic system, then into the bloodstream. Nutrients in the chyme are sent to all body parts to nourish and sustain your body, and also your mind.

The indigestible portion remains in the large intestines until expelled or eliminated in a bowel movement. But infrequent movements or longer periods of constipation result in a partial decomposition of these waste substances which are then reabsorbed by the bloodstream. This clutters up the entire circulatory system and leads to an unclean internal situation.

EARLY SYMPTOMS OF INTERNAL TOXEMIA

Retained poisons are sent to various body parts by your bloodstream in a valiant effort to get rid of these toxic substances.

Some of these substances accumulate to form boils, stones, pimples, and various other types of growths. The very early symptoms are usually sallow skin color, nervous irritability, coated tongue, bad breath, offensive body odor, headaches, bloating, a feeling of stomach heaviness and poor appetite.

"The putrefied mass in the intestines also forms gases which are absorbed partly into the bloodstream, causing more poisoning," says Dr. Irwin F. Krimm, author of *Health, Success And Happiness For You.* "Some of the gases are voided by the sufferer causing inconvenience, embarrassment and direct harm to the anus. Hemorrhoids (piles) and fistula of the anus are often caused by continual voiding of gases. These gases also back up from the intestines into the stomach, cause belching, and also pain, by distending the stomach and intestines."

The same toxic wastes come up into the mouth to cause bad odors and a sour taste which cannot be successfully camouflaged or eliminated by any of the breath remedies on the market.

Internal toxemia is responsible for poor appetite; a condition of clogged insides and fermented wastes is hardly conducive to a desire for healthful eating.

ADVANCED EFFECTS OF INTERNAL TOXEMIA

When the toxic wastes and debris substances are not removed, the sticky mass adheres to the walls of the large intestines, becoming solidified. More and more is added until the entire inner portion of these intestines resembles a thick tube with a slender open center channel through which the remains of undigested food must pass.

Among the poisonous gases that form are skatole, indole, ammonia, methylgadinine, mytilotoxin, sulphemoglobine. Others that later form include carbon dioxide, phenylpropionic and phenylacetic acids, marsh gas, and hydrogen sulphide, which can be corrosive and very damaging.

Catarrhal conditions of the lining of the intestinal tube further hinder digestive powers. Catarrh is a good example of internal toxemia because it is a covering of the intestinal lining with slime or mucous which slows up the secretion of digestive fluids and delays and reduces digestive powers.

HOW TOXEMIA MAY CAUSE COLITIS

Prolonged internal toxemia may lead to a condition of colitis — alternate constipation and diarrhea. The bacteria of putrefaction multiply with enormous rapidity in the delayed current of food waste matter passing down the bowel canal. Not only are more poisons produced that pass into the blood and burden the organs of elimination, but they irritate locally and set up an inflammatory condition in the bowel lining. This is just the start of internal toxemia.

HOW LAXATIVES CAN DAMAGE YOUR HEALTH

A middle-aged bank clerk is a laxative addict. He cares not a whit about cleaning out his insides by controlled fasting (a special plan will be given to you in the latter portion of this chapter) and reaches for tablets, powders and liquids.

"It's easy," he boasts, "when I take a tablet the night before. How often do I take laxatives? Oh, just about every other day."

How does he look and feel? He is rather pale, on the wan side, not too alert, and constantly feeling tired. He is only 41 but feels much older. "Guess my old age is creeping up on me," he smiles wryly.

Laxatives are draining out the health of this man, depleting his body of vital nutrients that are making him prematurely old and tired. Laxatives act by virtue of their irritating qualities. They punish the intestinal walls so that the body reacts with a shock, ejecting these laxatives as quickly as possible together with internal wastes. Repeated use of these laxatives will weaken the intestinal wall so that they cannot function without this violent laxative action. Other laxatives are dehydrators in that they draw water through the intestines (from other body parts where water may be needed) and dilute wastes to a near liquid state, creating diarrhea.

As for mineral oil (refined petroleum, actually), this lubricates and coats wastes with a slick layer so they can slip through the intestines. Mineral oil interferes with digestion and also the absorption of precious nutrients such as Vitamins A, D, and E.

The bank clerk described above is depleting his body of these precious nutrients by taking laxatives of all sorts, as well as mineral oil. If he went on a simple controlled fasting program, he could relieve constipation and be rid of the laxative habit permanently, with far better health.

FOODS TO ELIMINATE DURING FASTING

The controlled fasting plan to end intestinal distress calls for the elimination of refined foods such as all white bread, all refined grain products. Eliminate pastries, sweets, cakes, ice cream, malteds, all soft drinks, all spices, all condiments, all processed foods, all rich and all fried foods. Reduce intake of coffee and tea. Eliminate chocolate (certain ingredients in chocolate and foods containing chocolate have an inhibitory influence in that they cause a condition of constipation) and fried foods.

These foods create internal debris during the digestive process, and toxic extracts cling to the intestinal walls, clog the capillaries, block the passage of digested foods and extracted nutrients that must go into the bloodstream. Accumulations of these waste substances may remain for weeks and months and lead to a general feeling of depression, indigestion, belching, headaches, dizziness, brain fog, insomnia, etc. This gelatinous mass that can be truly termed garbage, can set up a serious internal chain reaction in undermining health.

Controlled fasting begins with elimination of these harmful foods as listed above.

WHY WATER DRINKING IS ESSENTIAL

Since the body is composed largely of water, its water supply must be replenished daily. Normally, four to eight glasses are needed each day. Water will put into solution the food nutrients that will then be absorbed and utilized by the body. Water softens the accumulated internal clutter of debris and helps in natural elimination.

UPON ARISING

Want to start the day off right? Upon arising, take two cups of hot water that has been flavored with freshly squeezed lemon juice.

Try teakettle tea — mix ¼ soya milk to ¾ boiled water. (Soya milk is available at most health food stores.) Drink upon arising. You will find that this flushes out your system and helps induce a bowel movement and passing off of much accumulated internal debris.

HOW A SCHOOLTEACHER'S FEAR OF LAXATIVES WAS OVERCOME

Miss Jenny taught grade school. Years of wrong dietary habits led to constipation. "I'm afraid of laxatives," she confided. "Suppose I take one at night, or in the morning, and then have to drive to school before anything happens. It can be very embarrassing, especially in the middle of a class. What can I do?"

I gave her this old-time remedy that has worked time and again for those who are faced with stubborn constipation and run the risk of accumulations of internal toxic wastes. Here is the remedy as I gave it to this schoolteacher.

Immediately upon arising in the morning, eat two large fresh apples, skin and all. Follow this with two glasses of freshly poured cold tap water. The action of the water upon the minerals and pectin and natural fruit acid of the apples will create a highly stimulating action upon sluggish bowels. Because of the strength of this natural remedy, it should be taken *only* in the morning and *only* upon an empty stomach, *before breakfast*.

Jenny tried it one morning, getting up two hours earlier to give it time to work. "It was wonderful," she confided. "It took just thirty minutes. Afterwards, I felt so light, so relieved, as if my entire insides had been washed clean."

Indeed, that is exactly what happened. This could not be the situation with harsh laxatives which create a habit and addiction.

CONTROLLED FASTING PLAN
FOR INTERNAL BODY HOUSECLEANING

The following foods leave very little poisonous wastes and have a cleansing action on the intestinal system.

BREAKFAST

Any kind of seasonal raw fruit together with any kind of a stewed fruit such as stewed peaches, stewed pears, baked apple, stewed prunes. Drink buttermilk or yogurt together with banana slices.

LUNCHEON

A raw vegetable salad. Baked steamed or boiled potato, yam or sweet potato, or corn on cob. Steamed natural brown rice. Whole wheat melba toast. Herb tea. (Sold at diet shoppes and health food stores.)

DINNER

Large helping of raw vegetables. Soft bland Italian ricotta cheese and a portion of lean fish or chicken, or lamb chops or lean meat with all visible fats trimmed off. Herb tea.

This controlled fasting plan helps clean out your insides and help build vibrant health. Could anything be simpler?

TRY THIS HEALTH SOUP

For three nights in a row, omit your evening meal. In its place, try this delicious soup. Cook together freshly ground whole wheat grains with chopped onion and a crushed garlic clove. Add some finely chopped parsley and a spoonful of pure olive oil. Take this soup with crisp or whole meal bread. It works wonders to clean out your insides. Ask for these foods at a grocery store or health food store.

SECRET OF HERBAL CLEANSERS

You may succeed in nullifying the toxic effects of intestinal debris by taking this herbal cleanser. Make an herbal infusion or soup such as senna pod or senna leaf tea, strain it and then add a sliced potato, including the skin, a teaspoon of bran, a teaspoon of linseeds and simmer for about 15 minutes. If you don't like the taste, strain it and just drink the liquid. Try this herbal cleanser both mornings and evenings. The ingredients are sold at most health food stores.

The secret here is that the alkaline content of the raw potato neutralizes certain toxic effect when combined with the senna pod or senna leaf tea, rich in revitalizing minerals.

CELLULOSE-RICH FOODS

Controlled fasting calls for elimination of toxic forming foods such as refined flour edibles which include macaroni, by the way, as well as mustard, pepper, ketchup, horse-radish. Avoid ice-cold beverages since these tighten the intestinal canal. At the same time, substitute for these cellulose rich foods that help form natural bulk that will pick up the gluey wastes and pass them off: figs, dates, dried peas, nuts, navy beans, raw tomatoes. Cantaloupes are important, as are watermelon and carrots, because their juice is needed to wash your insides effectively and dilute those toxic wastes that are to be drained out of your insides.

THE IMPORTANCE OF SIMPLE EXERCISE

In conjunction with your controlled fasting, you should carry out a simple exercise plan that helps stretch the inner organs. Here are some helpful ones:

1. In any position, alternately and vigorously draw in and bear down your stomach after you have let out all of your breath. Repeat 10 times.
2. Sit up from lying on your back. Repeat 10 times.
3. In a standing position, bend down at your waist (don't bend your knees!) and try to touch your toes. Repeat 10 times.

Internal toxemia is an unhealthy state that reaches a high point in constipation. Controlled fasting helps act upon clogged bowels to flush out impurities and restore the organism to its healthful and youthful birthright.

In Review:

1. Leftover waste residues in the intestinal canal give off gases and toxic substances that may lead to poor skin, coated tongue, bad breath, a feeling of bloating.
2. Laxatives are a crutch! They do not cure internal toxemia but may worsen the basic problem.
3. To flush out internal body inpurities, try the teakettle tea folk remedy, upon arising.
4. A stubborn case of constipation should react promptly to the apple-and-water remedy that is to be taken upon an empty stomach, before breakfast.
5. Fit the Controlled Fasting Plan into your daily menu. Try it for just one day and see the beneficial results.
6. Remember to avoid all spices, all condiments, all white flour and refined flour foods, including macaronies, sweets, cakes, pastries, candies, ice creams, etc. These all leave ash residue wastes that cling to the intestinal canal.
7. Try an herbal cleanser for a speedy internal housecleaning.
8. Step up the cellulose-containing food intake in your diet. These create natural bulk that will adhere to the residues and slough them off your insides.

5

How to Help Regulate Blood Pressure with Controlled Fasting

A pent-up, nervous and over-anxious executive heard that I was including a chapter on blood pressure in this book and rushed to place an advance order as he said, "I want to learn how I can live with my high blood pressure." I turned down his order and explained.

"My book is designed to tell people how to *get rid* of high blood pressure and live *without* it in health and happiness."

WHAT IS BLOOD PRESSURE?

Everyone has blood pressure. Without it, your body's blood could not circulate. Furthermore, blood pressure varies from moment to moment. It rises during excitement, it goes down during rest or sleep. These are normal changes. But when pressure goes higher than it should and stays that way, it means that something is wrong and something should be done about it.

Specifically, blood pressure is the force of blood against your artery walls. Your heart generates this pressure force as it beats or pumps. Your heart provides the pressure to keep blood moving through your arteries — the blood vessels that carry blood from the heart to all body parts.

The artery walls are muscular and elastic; they stretch and

expand to take the ups and downs of blood pressure. Whenever your heart beats or contracts (about 70 to 90 times a moment), blood pressure in your arteries increases; when your heart relaxes between beats, blood pressure goes down. Therefore, you have an "upper" and a "lower" blood pressure.

BLOOD PRESSURE READING

To read your blood pressure, your doctor uses a sphygmomanometer. He places an inflatable cuff around your arm just above the elbow. He fills this cuff with air by squeezing a rubber bulb. As the cuff gets tighter it compresses a large artery in your arm that temporarily closes off the blood flow through the artery because the squeeze from the air pressure in the cuff is more than the push of the blood in the artery.

At this point, the glass tube portion of this instrument which contains a column of mercury shows the mercury high up. The doctor starts to let the air out of the cuff and this causes the mercury to drop in the tube. He listens with his stethoscope on the compressed artery just below the cuff. When the air pressure in the cuff is a bit lower than the artery's blood pressure, blood starts to flow through the artery with each heartbeat. This rhythmic blood escapes beneath the cuff produces a distinct sound which your physician can hear with his stethoscope. When he hears this sound, he notes the height of the mercury. This is the *systolic* or "upper" pressure — the maximum pressure produced by your heart.

The physician continues to release air from the cuff until the moment when the distinct beating sound disappears as the blood is flowing more steadily through the artery. At this point, the height of the mercury shows the *diastolic* or "lower" pressure — the minimum pressure produced in the artery.

Generally, blood pressure is recorded by two figures. The systolic pressure is written first and then the diastolic — for instance, 130/90. This is read as "130 over 90." So you can see that everyone has blood pressure. Without it, life would cease! Too much of it can also end life! This is known as *high blood pressure* or *hypertension*.

High blood pressure may bring about other ailments such as stroke, heart disease, kidney trouble and hardening of the arteries.

WHO GETS HIGH BLOOD PRESSURE?

Those who are under conditions of stress, those whose blood-streams are carriers of toxic waste substances that must be removed are prime candidates. It is estimated that 1 out of every 20 adults has high blood pressure. Another 1 out of every 20 adults has high blood pressure in the early stages that will progress if not properly managed in time. The average age at onset is the early 30's.

Certain internal excitants create a condition of psychic tension that lead to short tempers, nervousness, extreme sensitivity that upset internal body balance and make the victim susceptible to influences that raise pressure. Toxic wastes may raise pressure. The kidneys, for example, may be overburdened with toxic substances and in an effort to wash themselves clean, issue *angiotonin,* an ingredient that raises blood pressure while endeavoring to get rid of toxic wastes. The endocrine glands also give off these self-cleansing substances in an effort to slough off internal toxemia and this may raise blood pressure, too.

EFFECTS OF HIGH BLOOD PRESSURE

A debris-ridden system affects the heart and blood vessels and other organs. These waste substances cling to the body's arteries and arterioles, shutting down, clamping them down, making it difficult for blood to get through to the capillaries. When this happens, your heart has to work harder to pump blood through the constricted vessels. To maintain blood flow, the heart muscle must grow larger and stronger. After a period of time, the heart's muscle fibers stretch. Eventually, the heart's own arteries cannot nourish this master organ and heart disease may ensue.

High blood pressure can lead to hardening of the arteries (arteriosclerosis) with varying degrees of damage. (Read Chapter 10 for further information.) Following this, the kidneys and brain may be injured. If a brain artery ruptures or closes, it leads to a "stroke."

A debris-filled bloodstream puts additional strain on the filtering system of the kidneys, results in the accumulation of body wastes in your internal rivers of life (bloodstream) causing *uremia*. This sets up a vicious cycle because the internal blood flow in the kidneys has an effect on the rest of the body's blood pressure.

EARLY WARNING SYMPTOMS

Headaches, dizziness, shortness of breath, light-headedness, vertigo, easy fatigue, frequent blushing (Nature is trying to release the steam exerted by debris-drenched blood by means of facial blushing), heart palpitation, bowel rumbling and perspiration (again, an effort by Nature to pass off, through skin pores, the accumulated wastes in the system) are some early warning symptoms.

Strokes are a possible complication of hypertension and the most severe consequence. Known as a *cerebral vascular accident* or an *intracranial lesion of vascular origin,* strokes are third among causes of death. Strokes are caused by the bursting of a blood vessel in the brain and sometimes by the clogging of an artery in the brain. Strokes appear as a sudden loss of consciousness (coma) followed by paralysis, generally on the body side opposite the side of the brain affected (hemiplegia). There may be paralysis of the face, arm or leg. Strokes are often advanced consequences of a condition of internal toxemia that initiates its evil influence by means of raising blood pressure that is preparatory to more serious consequences.

WHAT IS NORMAL PRESSURE?

Generally speaking, physicians feel that 100 plus age is normal. Others claim that 100 plus age up to 20 years, and then one point for every two years is acceptable. Since blood pressure varies with each individual and fluctuates in accordance with the varied influences that stimulate the heart and nervous system, there is no hard and fast rule, but a rule of thumb as per above — this is, 100 plus the age, etc.

The founder of the famous Battle Creek Sanitarium, Harvey Kellogg, M.D., at the age of 72, had a blood pressure reading of 118/80 and was pronounced fit as a fiddle.

OVERWEIGHT IS HARMFUL

Accumulated wastes often accompany overweight. (See Chapter 8 for more about this.) Dr. Louis I. Dublin, Chief Statistician of the Metropolitan Life Insurance Company, stated, "A recent study among employees of the Company showed that elevation of the blood pressure was more than twice as frequent at ages 45 to 54 and three times as frequent at the ages of 35 to 44 among those of heavy build as among those of light build." Overweight is regarded more serious in the 35 to 44 groups. Years of retaining toxic wastes, years of building up weight and excess fat that is composed of accumulated poisonous substances, all give rise to increased blood pressure.

FRUIT IS NATURE'S OWN REMEDY FOR ABNORMAL PRESSURE

Fresh, raw fruits help the body to *dissolve* and to *metabolize* the internal toxic wastes that are carried by the bloodstream and lead to conditions of hypertension or high blood pressure. This has been seen by Dr. Alice Chase who reports:

> The sufferer from high blood pressure must be put on the kind of food that will bring about intensive elimination from the cells and the fluids of accumulated metabolic wastes. I have used a raw-fruit dietary which is the only type of dietary that can bring about remarkable changes from disease symptoms to normal health.
>
> This can happen only when the sufferer is kept for a long time on a fruit diet and very little else. The fruits must be raw and fresh. The sub-acid fresh fruits should be the main staples when they can be obtained — apricots, peaches, cherries and the citrus fruits such as pineapples, oranges and grapefruits. Perseverance with a fruit diet for several weeks works wonders. Not only does the blood pressure come down, it stays down!

The high blood pressure victim should set aside three days and devote these to fruit intake entirely. Gradually, reduce other foods and substitute raw and fresh fruits in singular or salad form, drink freshly extracted juices, during other days of the week. When you are able to do so, devote seven full days to fruit eating. You will find that the internal wastes will be sloshed away by the rich nutrient-carrying juices of fruits.

Occasionally, have one day in which you skip *all* meals, drinking only fresh fruit and vegetable juices.

A DOCTOR'S CONTROLLED FASTING PLAN

Here is a controlled fasting plan as suggested by Owen S. Parrett, M. D., in *The Golden Age* (Vol. LXXX, No. 11):

> So far as possible, avoid big dinners at night. If you are retired, have your main dinner about one o'clock or, better still, two o'clock. Have only fruit at night, or a hot drink of Breakfast Cup (sold at health stores) or some other cereal coffee, or perhaps a bowl of home-made vegetable soup without meat or meat stock.
>
> Fruit I prefer to all else! A large fruit salad makes a delightful evening meal, and its Viatmin C will help bring your clotting tendencies down and at the same time strengthen the walls of your blood vessels, decreasing their fragility. If you are still punching a clock, have a substantial lunch and an early light supper.

9-STEP PLAN

Dr. Parrett also adds that a spasm of the arteries of the brain is a frequent cause of both false and real strokes. As the arteries go into spasm, clots may more easily form so that the spasms may play a leading role in causing permanent brain damage. How to help avoid spasms? Here is the doctor's own 9-step plan:

1. Eat less.
2. Exercise more.
3. Take enough and frequent vacation periods or chances to relax and forget shop, business and your many problems.
4. Make fruit a big factor in your diet.
5. Keep away from sugar largely, avoiding gooey sweet desserts.
6. Cut coffee, tea and meat out of your diet.
7. Eat few if any eggs. Get your protein from the vegetable kingdom mostly.
8. Avoid big late dinners.
9. Keep a clear conscience before God and man.

GARLIC: INTERNAL CLEANSER

A recent discovery is that garlic exerts an internal cleansing and detoxification action comparable to that of penicillin. A European physician, G. Piotrowski, found that ordinary garlic has an internal antiseptic action on the toxic substances that cling to the arterial system and inhabit the bloodstream that may result with impaired blood pressure function. Dr. Piotrowski treated numerous patients and successfully lowered their high blood pressure by giving them ordinary garlic! No other treatments were given. After garlic detoxified the bloodstream, it worked to dilate the blood vessels, permit a normal blood flow and thereby serve to regulate normal blood pressure.

Dr. Piotrowski reported that many patients were relieved of such symptoms as: headaches, dizziness, angina-like pains, ringing in the ears, pains in the back between the shoulder blades. All this was accomplished by giving the patients ordinary garlic, either in cloves or extracted oil.

Garlic is rich in Vitamins A, B and especially C as well as the precious minerals of manganese, copper, zinc, sulfur, iron, calcium, chlorine, etc. These nutrients work together to act as a *carminative* — internal cleansing action, nullifying the toxic wastes, sweeping these wastes from the system and helping normalize blood pressure and general health.

To your controlled fasting plan of fruit, add garlic. Chop and dice and mix in salads. Try garlic perles (sold at health stores) that leave no volatile essence on your breath. Munch garlic with parsley to avoid social hazards.

DIGESTIVE ACIDITY, GAS, HEARTBURN

You feel the accumulated effects of internal toxemia with a burning sensation in your esophagus (food tube), which passes near the heart in its passage from stomach to throat. Heartburn, by the way, has nothing to do with your heart. It is thus named because you feel this hyperacidity in your chest region. Here is a controlled fasting home remedy to cleanse out the toxic waste residues that cause excess acid in your system.

Grate a raw potato finely, fold the pulp into a cheesecloth, and press out the juice. Dilute this with three times the amount of warm water and take this regularly *first thing in the morning,* before lunch and before retiring at night. It is best to prepare it fresh each time. Note that you can continue eating but you precede each of your three meals with this home remedy. To hinder the formation of excess acid waste residues, abstain from excessively flavored and spiced dishes and eliminate white sugar and white flour products.

Uncooked oatflakes, well-chewed and insalivated, will also help wash out the toxic wastes that have accumulated in your esophagus and cause distress.

The alkaline content of the raw potato helps neutralize acidity. The well-chewed oatflakes help wash out the waste substances of internal toxemia.

HOW AN ADVERTISING COPYWRITER HANDLES JOB TENSION

The world of advertising can be quite hectic, lots of push-push-push. But it's a creative world and appeals to the creatively inclined person. That was Sidney, a bright young copywriter who was faced with rush-rush-rush deadlines, harrowing conferences with clients, often harsh criticisms. "My blood pressure really soared," he complained. "I'd get those pounding headaches, break out in sweats, feel my heart slamming in my chest. I used to reach for a smoke. After a while, I became such a tobacco addict, I would chainsmoke and my pressure almost exploded." (Tobacco is a crutch and offers no benefits. More about this in Chapter 7.) "A photographer told me he once did a picture spread for a garlic company and heard that this food can clean out the insides. I tried it. Now, when I feel nervous and tense, I reach for a garlic perle in the office. At home, I eat diced garlic with raw vegetable salads every night."

The results? The company doctor said his blood pressure went down and is generally satisfactory. Young Sidney has been able to ease up on his smoking urge, too, as a result.

USE OF SALT DURING FASTING

This harsh condiment contains sodium chloride, a chemical that whips up internal upheaval, leaves an ash residue that clings to the vascular walls, is seen mingled in the bloodstream and raises the pressure.

Two prominent doctors in pursuing their experiments have found that those who are on a low-salt or salt-free diet have either slightly high or normal blood pressure. Those who are on a high-salt diet are invariably victims of high blood pressure. The doctors wrote, "In view of the foregoing considerations, it is proposed that the level of sodium intake is the primary etiological factor (cause) in the development of essential hypertension."

"I MUST HAVE SALT!"

This was the declaration made by a too-stout, too-nervous housewife in her late 40's and already showing a too-high blood pressure reading. "I just can't enjoy food without salt and my doctor put me on a salt-free diet." She was on the verge of tears. "Maybe it's just habit, but I must have salt. What'll I do?"

Her neighbor suggested she go into any health store or diet shop and buy some of the salt substitutes — many are made from certain vegetables and have a pseudo-salt taste but are absolutely free of sodium chloride. Expert salt addicts are often fooled when eating dishes prepared with salt substitutes.

The housewife tried it and now she said, "I must have salt — that is, salt substitute!"

A SALT-FREE DIET

Certain substances in salt and salt-containing foods become liberated when subjected to the enzymatic and digestive processes. These substances create ash residues that cling with a "magnetic" action to the arterial walls and circulatory systems, causing blood pressure elevation. A salt-free diet is a simple controlled fasting plan that enables you to eat delicious foods but without salt content.

Salt-containing foods include potato chips, pickles, pretzels, canned meats, processed meats, biscuits, refined bread, caviar, processed cheeses, clams, olives, oysters, paprika, black pepper, and all brined, corned, pickled, smoked and salted foods.

Controlled fasting for control of high blood pressure calls for either reduction or elimination of these foods. *Read the labels* of canned goods and packages of other foods that you buy. If these foods contain salt, reduce intake. Step up your fresh fruit and vegetable intake, use fresh meats and non-processed cheeses, freshwater fish (nothing that comes from a can unless the label reads something to the effect of being low-sodium) and fresh poultry.

Yes, there is hope for your high blood pressure. Hope in bringing it down to a normal level. Controlled fasting helps to sweep away internal debris and toxic wastes so that you can live with normal blood pressure.

Main Points of Chapter 5

1. We all have blood pressure. Outer influences coupled with inner toxic influences conspire to wreck normal blood pressure levels. Tension is another villain.
2. Accumulations of waste materials within the blood system lead to elevated pressure that may, in turn, predispose to conditions of hardening of the arteries, kidney and brain damage, a serious stroke.
3. Familiarize yourself with the early warning symptoms that may be traced to a debris-filled bloodstream.
4. Fresh, raw fruits exert a miraculous power in dissolving and metabolizing internal toxic wastes. Try controlled fasting on a fruit diet.
5. Fit the 9-step plan into your schedule for a period of two weeks.
6. Garlic is a "magic" food that detoxifies your bloodstream and helps reduce blood pressure.
7. Eliminate salt in all forms.
8. Eat fresh foods in all forms to nourish your system and combat internal bacteria.

6

How a Raw Juice Fast
Can Banish Internal
Body Poisons

The first and fifteenth day of every month is a special occasion for me. Both are my housecleaning days. The house that is cleaned from top to bottom, inside and out, is my body. These two days are circled on my calendar and are rarely changed. Cleaning house — cleaning out my body poisons — has helped improve and sustain my personal health, body and mind. Internal stomach and digestive toxic agents are sloshed out of my system when I embark upon this anticipated housecleaning.

This is not just "dusting off" the surfaces. Rather, my special plan cleans out the crevices and nooks, washing out the deepest recesses of my insides. You may think that I refer only to elimination. This is just a partial segment of my internal housecleaning plan. My special RJF (raw juice fast) method not only washes out my intestines, but also my lungs, my kidneys, my skin, my endocrine system, my organs of perception (eyes, ears, nose, etc.) and my thinking facilities, too.

This RJF plan works to combat the retention of toxins that stagnate my insides. For instance, the lungs breathe in oxygen and expel carbon dioxide which is a poison, some of which clings to the tissues of the bronchial system. The kidneys serve to eliminate the toxic by-products of metabolism and in the various nooks and crevices of these organs will be found residue. The skin has a vast network of porous sweat glands through which are expelled poisonous wastes and gases, yet particles do remain that must be washed off — inside as well as outside. The intestinal tract is still another organ that serves to rid the body of toxemia yet becomes clogged up with particles and offensive substances. All of these organs work at top efficiency if results are to be obtained.

RJF — *the raw juice fast* — is my special technique for washing out my insides and I will presently tell you how you can benefit from this unique discovery.

AN RJF WORKING SCHEDULE

On the first and fifteenth day of each month, my controlled fasting plan calls for elimination of food and substitution of freshly squeezed raw fruit and vegetable juices. It is a comparatively easy plan to follow when you decide it will help your health and when you discover the completely marvelous feeling of rejuvenation and lightness that follow this method. You may shake your head and say, "Oh, it's easy for this fellow, Mr. Wade, to follow such a plan. He sits home all the time, can make his own juices in his kitchen, a few steps away from his study. But what about me? I have to go to work every day."

Let me enlighten you. I go to work every day, too, yet I adhere to my RJF plan with simplicity, year in and year out. My own health has become so supercharged and revitalized, I wouldn't swap these two days for anything.

Five days a week, I go to my New York City office where I keep regular hours as a working literary agent. In addition to representing writers, I manage to turn out close to a million words a year in my own writing. I write extensively on nutrition, work with food companies in preparing health articles, edit a health magazine, write a syndicated column — *Country Kitchen* — that appears in a magazine distributed in nearly 700 health stores throughout the country. Deadlines are many. Publication schedules go awry, publishers and advertisers are fickle and call me to make last minute schedules. Then there are luncheons, occasional dinners, a few social activities as well as endless conferences. Through it all, I have never altered my RJF plan because I prepare for it a day in advance, tell myself that no matter what happens, no matter where

I eat, I will specify that this is my day for internal housecleaning and will order freshly squeezed raw fruit or vegetable drinks for my meals. With this attitude and perseverance, I have enjoyed renewed health and vigor. If this were not so, I could never keep up my busy schedule and love every minute of it. In fact, most of my weekends are spent at home where I turn out reams of articles and stories and books. This book that you are now reading was written at home during weekends and holidays.

I am a dedicated believer in natural health and follow my own dictates. It would be impossible for me to maintain such a schedule, often a seven-day-a-week writing schedule, if I were not in such tip top health. And I credit my special RJF plan for restoring me to such good health and vibrancy. Yes, I say "restoring" because prior to my discovery about the remarkable healing values of controlled fasting, I fell victim to numerous ailments.

Work pressure gave me blinding headaches and migraine attacks that were merciless. To someone who must exert mental effort, migraine is tortuous. Constant deadlines tied up my stomach in knots and my food remained like lumps in my stomach. My complexion was sallow. Cramps became a hated part of my life. Insomnia made me grouchy. My nerves were stretched as taut as a string. There were times when I wanted to give up everything and run off into the woods and hide myself from civilization. (I did this for two weeks but the isolation was more than I could bear. It did give me time to think and decide that while I could not change the world, I could change my own health and resistance, build it up to meet the challenge of the outside.)

HOW TO FAST ON JUICES
ACCORDING TO MOTHER NATURE

During my two week runaway, I occupied a little shack in the mountains. My store of provisions ran low. A local bridge leading to a nearby village had become washed out so I faced the prospect of swimming across (impossible) or starving (not impossible, but undesirable). While strolling through the dense woods, I nearly stepped upon something. I should say, "someone." When I saw him, I was startled. He looked like Rip Van Winkle with a long flowing beard and a cherub-looking face. His clothes were neatly patched and very clean. He was awake at once, bounded to his feet like a youth, shook my hand and beamed,

"Glad to have a visitor. Come on along and let's chat."

Startled, I went along with him to his little shack overlooking a bubbling brook. Surrounded by thick pine and fir trees, birds chirping, the wind whispering, it was Eden come to life. Could this be real? I wondered. It most certainly was.

"Do you live here, all alone?" I asked when I sat down on a makeshift chair in his neat cabin, sparse with only utilitarian furniture, but swept clean and neat. "Just how do you manage to survive?"

"Easy — I live according to Mother Nature. I survive quite well on fruits and vegetables. Some grow wild. Others I plant myself. Once in a while I go to the village, buy other supplies, a little meat. I catch fish in the brook. But mostly, I depend upon Mother Nature."

Then he told me about himself. He had been a successful attorney in the city for many years. The pressure was too great for him. He was a heavy smoker, liked to drink, addicted to sweets and starches. He had been overweight, susceptible to heart trouble (had two minor attacks) and developing diabetes, not to mention stiff fingers that suggested arthritis.

"I figured we have only one life to live — why not live it well? I took a leave of absence for seven months, found this place and here I am. My seven month period is almost over. I'll go back to my law firm, but weekends, I'll come here, live on raw juices so I can revitalize my system." He fingered his beard. "This'll have to go, of course, but it's what's *inside* a man that counts. And I healed my insides, cleaned them out, got rid of the toxic agents, wastes, poisons, and feel reborn. Would you believe it — I'm 53, and feel like I'm 23?"

He did look young. Then I grinned as I said, "I'm 23 — but I feel like 53 — and that's the truth. Say, I'm hungry and was wondering about getting to the Village to buy some food. The bridge is washed out."

"Lucky thing it is," was his reply. "Otherwise, you'll be feeling like 63 and then 73 if you don't go back to Nature. Tell you what, let me feed you — that's right — you'll eat what I give you to eat. Try it for three days. Then you decide whether you want to live according to Nature or according to Man."

THREE DAY RJF FAST

For a period of three days, I lived on freshly squeezed raw fruit and vegetable juices. The two of us would crank an old-fashioned hand juicer (no electricity in the woods) and drink the delicious beverages, combinations, mixes. By the end of the third day, I felt years younger — many years younger.

"You've sold me on Nature," was my parting praise when it came time to go back to the city. "I forgot about Nature and paid the penalty for wrong living."

That chance meeting altered the course of my life, led to the discovery of controlled fasting, awakened me to the dangers of internal toxemia, digestive upset traced to toxic waste residues, and the miracle of a *raw juice fast*. I have adhered to eating natural foods in a natural manner. Twice each month, on the first and fifteenth, I enjoy internal housecleaning. If I go to lunch or dinner with business associates, publishers or writers, on these particular days, I explain that I'm on this RJF plan and order juices — singly, or in combination.

COMPLETE REJUVENATION POSSIBLE

This special controlled fasting technique got rid of internal poisons to the point where today I am free from those punishing migraine headaches, have better vision, enjoy strong nerves, a pleasant disposition (much to the relief of my co-workers), sleep like a log nightly, have a light-feeling stomach, walk tall, feel tall, think tall. I could hardly keep up my rigorous schedule that calls for writing one million words yearly and editing another million, not to mention library research, interviews, etc., conferences and deadlines, if I were not in tip-top shape.

You, too, may walk the pathway of Nature's Health by cleansing your insides with raw juices and vegetables. Squeeze them at home with an extractor. Most department stores and health food stores sell them. Select restaurants, if you must eat out, that serve freshly squeezed juices. Ask the headwaiter. If you eat in at your job, bring along a thermos or two of freshly squeezed juices.

CLEANSING POWER OF RAW FRUIT JUICES

Fruit juices give your body the needed glycogen for the maintenance of fats and body warmth. The detoxification elements in raw juices aid in sustaining the chemical composition and metabolic balance of your bloodstream; these same detoxification elements help to assimilate substances in your tissues and prevent excess cellular congestions caused by waste product accumulations. Natural carbons present in fruit juices generate your cerebro-vital functions, casting off accumulated debris, relieving the effects of a high-tensioned nervous life.

CLEANSING CONSEQUENCES

The British Ministry of Health has stated, "Juices are valuable in relief of hypertension, cardiovascular and kidney diseases and obesity. Good results have also been obtained in rheumatic, degenerative and toxic states. Juices have an all-around protective action. Good results can be obtained when large amounts up to one quart daily are taken in treatment of peptic ulceration, also in treatment of chronic diarrhea, colitis and toxemia of gastro and intestinal origin. The high buffering capacities of the juices reveal that they are very valuable in the treatment of hyperchlorhydria. Milk has often been used for this purpose but . . . juices were far superior to milk for this purpose."

BENEFITS ABOUT VEGETABLE JUICES

In raw vegetable juices, we have a tremendous treasure of minerals, those detoxifying agents that clean out the lining surfaces of the digestive system, bring about oxidation of wastes in the tissues. Vegetable juices and their minerals create an alkalinizing condition so that "acidosis" is overcome and the accumulated body toxins are prepared for elimination and given off, thrown out of the body.

The power of minerals is explained comprehensively in my volume, *Magic Minerals: Key to Better Health.*[1] Ask for this book at any bookshop or health food store. If it's sold out, place an order with them or request an order blank from the publishers.

WHAT HAPPENS DURING RJF FAST PLAN

A one-day Raw Juice Fast plan should do the following, considering that your impaired health has been brought about through abnormal composition of the blood and accumulation of toxic wastes in the system:

1. RJF will give your entire organism a rest. Your stomach and intestinal tracts will become emptied and relieved.
2. Blood pressure is lowered, pulse becomes more stable. Body temperature is also normalized. The entire body metabolism enjoys a rest, comparable to that of a deep and healthful sleep.
3. The stomach and intestinal linings which ordinarily act as a sponge for the absorption of food materials, begin to eliminate toxic matter from your system.
4. Stored up starch, glycogen and fat will be used up to feed the body. Protein tissues now go to work to provide heat and needed energy.
5. RJF is a part of controlled fasting that gives your vital organs a rest and permits the inherent healing influences an opportunity to perform their work without interference.

YOUR RJF PROGRAM:

Breakfast: Glass of prune and fig juice into which has been stirred a tablespoon of apple cider vinegar. Glass of pear juice. After one hour, a cup of yogurt (a creamy liquid but a liquid, nevertheless, and therefore permissible) together with wheat germ flakes.

---

[1] Carlson Wade, *Magic Minerals: Key to Better Health* (West Nyack, New York: Parker Publishing Company, 1967).

Luncheon: Glass of tomato juice. After 15 minutes, a glass of lettuce, cucumber and beet juice. Dessert may be the juice of stewed apricots.

Dinner: Celery, radish and lettuce juice. Wait 15 minutes and enjoy a glass of carrot juice. After 15 more minutes, a glass of cabbage juice to which has been added one tablespoon of green pepper juice.

Personally, I follow this plan on the first and fifteenth of every month and my only variation is the selection of fruits and vegetables. Select seasonable fruits and vegetables, organically grown. Ask your health food store for the name and address of a local supplier. Or, write to the Department of Agriculture in your State Capital for the name and address of a farmer who can supply organically grown produce. Many such farmers sell through the mail. You may drive to their farm if you wish, depending upon your circumstances. I buy my organically grown produce from a health store in New York City that receives daily supplies from a nearby farm. I pick up my produce on my way home from work.

PURIFYING POWERS OF SPECIFIC FRUITS

You may be interested in the specific internal cleansing actions of specific fruits and may want to emphasize them in your one-day RJF plan.

Apples — rich in maltic acid which helps clear out debris that may cause internal inflammation.

Berries — all are rich in iron and calcium that exert a cleansing influence upon the blood stream.

Coconuts — rich in precious minerals that ease stomach and liver ailments.

Figs — seeds have an undefined substance that works upon the intestines, cleansing this system, aiding in elimination.

Grapes — juice is rich in vitamins and minerals to clean the bloodstream and nourish the red cells.

Lemons — prime source of hesperidin and Vitamin C that neutralize acid wastes in the system.

Oranges — another mineral source that helps attack toxic wastes in nooks and crevices.

Peaches — vitamins and minerals dissolve toxic wastes close to the skin surface, helping to build a skin that is as pretty as a peach.

Pineapples — source of bromelin which acts upon the pancreas and cleans out this insulin-forming organ.

Plums — vitamins as well as minerals such as silicon and sulphur cleanse out toxemia in the body organs.

Strawberries — detoxifies the bloodstream, helps conditions of acidosis, catarrh, nervous upsets.

PURIFYING POWERS OF RAW VEGETABLE JUICES

Here are a few of the more popular vegetables and their housecleaning powers.

Alfalfa — forms alkali, maintains the acid-alkaline body ratio. Has amino acids that wash out body cells and tissues, rejuvenating them.

Artichoke — contains natural insulin that is hydrolized to levulose by acid and cleanses the nervous system.

Asparagus — rich in minerals and Vitamin A to cleanse the arterial structures.

Beet — cleanses the bloodstream and stimulates a clean lymphatic flow throughout the circulatory system.

Broccoli — helps cleanse the water (more than 70%) in your body.

Cabbage — juices exert a beneficial influence upon the digestive system, cleansing the lining of the stomach.

Celery — helps the body dispose of carbon dioxide waste substances.

Endive — cleanses the intestines and liver.

Kale — helps slough off wastes and build healthy hair and skin.

Lettuce — wonderful for washing the stomach and neutralizing toxic agents in the acid-alkaline balance.

Mushroom — contains ingredients that help cleanse the bloodstream.

Mustard Greens — substances repair the capillaries and wash out the millions of body cells and tissues.

Okra — good for colitis and intestinal clutters.

Peas — rich protein and mineral supply, works upon toxic agents in the digestive and gastric tracts.

Peppers — the prime silicon source gets rid of toxic accumulations that erupt as boils, blemishes, skin and fingernail discolorations.

Radishes — magnesium soothes the nervous system and cleanses the digestive system by means of its sulphur content.

Tomato — highly alkaline, tomatoes wash out the stomach, neutralize excessive acidity.

There are many more fruits and vegetables which will help you. You may create your own combinations of beverages to suit your individual tastes. Personally, I prefer a breakfast of fruit juices exclusively, lunch of vegetable juices, dinner of vegetable juices and then a nightcap of a fruit juice. You may make up your own variations. *Don't combine fruit and vegetable juices because of ambivalent enzymatic actions.* The story of proper combinations and enzymatic power is found in my volume, *Helping Your Health with Enzymes.*

HOW TO PREPARE FOR YOUR RJF

Mentally prepare yourself by arranging to abstain from solids for this one day. Condition yourself to a day of juices. Re-read this chapter to see what health benefits you will derive from internal housecleaning. If you like company, ask a friend or relative or a co-worker to join with you in this RJF. Sometimes, there is no "making a deal" with Nature. You must live according to the rules of Mother Nature and cleanse out your insides. No compromises, no middle-of-the-way — the choice is yours.

Stimulating Points of this Chapter

1. RJF or *raw juice fast* is a one-day plan to wash out your insides. You live exclusively on fresh raw fruit and vegetable juices.
2. The author of this book maintains a schedule of producing close to one million words yearly by means of health improvement and clean insides. Prior to his discovery of the purifying powers of raw juices, he was ailing, prematurely aged and ready to quit everything. A successful future might have been lost if he had not found out about raw juices. This discovery is passed on to you in complete detail.

3. You may try a three day RJF controlled fasting plan with great
   benefit.
4. Raw juices help to get rid of internal poisons, contain detoxification
   and purifying substances, give you bountiful mental and physical
   health.
5. The entire human organism undergoes internal housecleaning with
   raw juices. Yes, *you can wash out your insides* by means of a simple
   and delicious one day *raw juice fast* plan.
6. Alternate between freshly squeezed raw fruit juices and raw vegetable juices.
7. Try RJF for one day — on the first and fifteenth of every month.
   You may increase it to two or three days in a row, depending upon
   your own needs.

7

How to Stop Smoking
with Controlled Fasting

Smoking is here to stay! Cigarettes, cigars, pipes, chewing tobacco, roll your owns — by any other name, tobacco is here to stay! All the threats, all the cancer scares, all the fears are *not* going to eliminate tobacco. If one million people, right now, were to quit smoking, within an hour another million people would start smoking, maybe more. Tobacco is a narcotic and exerts a drugged influence upon the smoker who cannot easily shake off the habit. The situation is not hopeless. If you *want* to stop smoking, if you are sincerely interested in getting rid of the habit, then this chapter will help you.

If, however, you have the attitude of my father (a chain smoker from the age of 13) that you want to keep on smoking until you die (and that is what killed him!) then skip over this chapter. You have nothing to lose. You have already lost it — your basic health.

Controlled fasting is a method of dietary improvement, proper substitutions of certain foods, elimination of offending substances and correct living habits. When these principles are followed, you can cleanse out toxic agents in your system and help recuperate your health birthright.

Controlled fasting is a *complete* system. You cannot use one phase of it in extract and hope to enjoy maximum good health. For instance, don't expect to have really clean insides by following every point in this book — and then reach for a smoke! Tobacco introduces nicotine, tars, a score of poisonous substances into the system that adhere, cling to, absorb and infect the billions of body cells, creating a chain reaction of toxemia that undermines all health.

SMOKER'S COUGH

A cough is a symptom of accumulated clutter of poisons in the respiratory system. Nature makes you cough in an effort to expel these waste substances. Smoker's cough is a steady warning signal that continued application of nicotine and tar are destroying the respiratory tissues.

Ever since I can remember, since my early childhood, my father had a hacking smoker's cough. It got on my nerves. It drove my mother out of the house for hours on end. But my father, an habitual smoker since the age of 13, could not and did not want to give up the smoking habit. In fact, he was such a tobacco addict, he was never without a cigarette in his mouth.

Years and years of coughing did take their toll. His lungs became infected. The air sacs expanded. Toxemia took effect and emphysema began to take over. He continued smoking. He took to his bed. He grew weaker and weaker. Before my eyes, he wasted away. He *did* stop smoking when he was so weak he could not hold up his yellowed fingers to grasp a cigarette. Medical house calls were to no avail. He was too far gone. In the end, an ambulance took him to the hospital. The attending physician took one look at him and even before asking for identification, asked my mother, "Was he a heavy smoker all his life?"

Be not deluded, as I said earlier. Smoking *is* here to stay. The only hope is that a doctor-prepared controlled fasting plan (which I'll outline to you in a few more pages) can help you.

NOT EASY TO QUIT

Mark Twain's famous witticism, "Quitting tobacco is simple. I've done it a hundred times," is good for a laugh but offers no help to the tobacco addict.

According to the National TB Association in its publication, *Cigarette Smoking: The Facts,*

The more cigarettes a person smokes, the more likely he is to die early. The earlier in life a person stops smoking, the more likely he is to die early. But ... a person who has stopped smoking is much safer than a person who smokes cigarettes.

Cigarette smokers are hooked — emotionally and physically. Many no longer enjoy smoking. They hate the after-taste, the messiness, the smell on their clothes and breath. They are also afraid. Most cigarette smokers wish — sometimes desperately — they had never started. Some of them are able to stop without too much trouble. But for others the attempt to stop may be hard. Quitting may involve days or weeks of jangling nerves, uncontrollable rage or weeping and physical discomfort ranging all the way from shaky fingers to severe fits of coughing.

Many people do quit smoking, despite the torture of breaking the habit. They want to do everything they can to live fully the long life that modern medical science has made possible. Their way — cutting cigarettes out completely — is the only way to protect health.

GOVERNMENT WARNINGS

The Surgeon General's Advisory Committee on Smoking and Health has officially blamed smoking for these ailments: lung cancer, bronchitis, heart diseases, cancer, ulcers, liver cirrhosis, premature babies. "Cigarette smoking is a health hazard," says the Committee, "of sufficient importance in the U.S. to warrant appropriate remedial action.

5-DAY STOP-SMOKING PLAN

In an effort to help people stop smoking, numerous physicians have banded together and formed special sessions. These are known as the Five-Day Plan To Stop Smoking. (They may be in existence in your town. Ask your local Health Department.) There are 10 basic rules that are based on a sound physiological principle designed to cleanse your insides and wash out debris and help you kick the habit. Before you begin, decide that you have had enough of nicotine. You want to stop. And you *must* stop if you want this special 10-Step-Plan to work. You stop at once, not piecemeal.

Remember, you are going to break a habit of 10, 20 or even 30 more years. You need strong willpower. Without willingness, this may not work. Here are the 10 rules as followed by those who attend these clinics:

1. Enjoy luxury. Take a warm bath two or three times a day for 15 or 20 minutes. Relax. If you have a sudden urge to smoke, hop back into the shower. You can't smoke in a shower.

2. Drink up to 8 glasses of water between meals. Keep a record if necessary. The more liquids you can down, the quicker nicotine is washed out of your body. Take no alcoholic beverages, no beer, no wine.

3. Get sufficient rest during this 5-day plan. Have regular meal times and a set time to go to bed. No night clubbing. You want to conserve nervous energy.

4. After each meal, get outside. Walk and breathe deeply for 30 minutes. Do not sit in your favorite chair after eating. This time is tempting for smoke. Your chair, curtains, rugs, clothes are all saturated with tobacco. Get away from them. Wear fresh garments. Get outside in fresh air.

5. Drink no alcohol, no tea, no coffee, no cola beverage. Avoid all sedatives and stimulants. Build up your nervous reserves. For a hot drink, try Postum or cereal beverages. Milk or buttermilk is good, too. Fruit and vegetable juices, too.

6. During these five days, avoid fish, fowl and meat. Avoid rich gravy, fried food, condiments and rich desserts. Omit candy, cake, pie and ice cream. For some reason, smoking is stimulated by foods that are highly spiced and saturated with pepper and mustard. Meat and rich foods are also akin with the smoking urge.

7. Eat all you want of fruit, grains, vegetables, legumes, nuts. Eat much fresh fruit.

8. You'll need to strengthen your nerves. At each meal, take two tablespoonfuls of wheat germ sold at all health stores. Take two tablespoonfuls daily of dried brewer's yeast with milk or tomato juice. Yeast concentrate (Vegex, Sovex, Savita, Marmite — sold at health stores) in hot water is also good.

9. After meals, rinse your mouth with one-half or one-fourth of 1 percent solution of silver nitrate. Do *not* swallow any of this solution because it is nearly as poisonous as nicotine. But it nullifies the taste for tobacco. You'll need a doctor's prescription for this solution. Tablets of silver nitrate are now available.

10. Ask God to help you. Place your will on God's side and you are invincible. You will succeed when you take God as your partner.

A DOCTOR'S ADVICE ON THIS FAST

J. Wayne McFarland, M.D., who helped formulate this plan, suggests you keep telling yourself that you do not choose to smoke. Deep-breathe. Walk for a glass of water when the urge hits you. This break helps lessen the urge. Continually breathe deeply when you feel the urge and the struggle is eased.

These moments of intense craving will become less pronounced, farther spaced in intervals.

Dr. McFarland adds, "The reason you must avoid coffee, tea, and cola beverages is that the effect of caffeine is to stimulate the nerves, the very nerves that crave nicotine. A cup of coffee is likely to call for a cigarette; beware this trap. The same goes for alcohol. Although alcohol is a depressant drug, it works on the same nerves that are trying to get rid of nicotine.

"The taboo on sweets during this 5-day period is to conserve your Vitamin B_1 (thiamine) reserves. Thiamine is the vitamin required for smooth nerves. Sugar robs you of B_1. Later on, after you have a good grip on the problem of tobacco, simple desserts and even pie or ice cream are all right, occasionally."

Why no flesh food? During this stress time, cholesterol blood levels are raised. Meat contains saturated fat which increases cholesterol. Meat contains purine bodies and ammonia which can act as stimulants to nerves. This is a time when you want to calm down nerves so eliminate meat, fish, fowl during this period.

A SECRETARY'S SUCCESS

At one of these special 5-Day clinics, a secretary from Des Moines, Iowa, reported she was a heavy chain smoker, at least two packs of cigarettes daily. Three days after following the plan to the letter, she could taste her food and enjoy scents again. She quit smoking entirely and later reported she could work better. Her brain was getting more oxygen and could function more efficiently.

A LAWYER'S SUCCESS

After smoking for 35 years, a Canadian lawyer broke the habit after attending this special clinic and following the 10-point plan. He reported, "I was desperate. The habit had such a hold on me that I would smoke 4 cigarettes before and 3 during breakfast. I was chain-smoking 60 to 70 cigarettes a day. That's 3½ packs or the equivalent of a cigarette 21 feet long. I figured my 30 years' indulgence had cost me $10,000." He began when he was 14.

He tried everything. It failed. The group therapy idea, the 24-hour fruit-juice controlled fasting, the faith in God — all helped break the habit. Now he is happy and healthy.

POWER OF CONTROLLED FASTING

As you can see, the stop-smoking plan utilizes the principles of controlled fasting, the washing out of the grime-filled insides and elimination of certain foods. The plan cleanses your insides, strengthens your will, removes your temptation, gives you inner strength to battle the foe that is tobacco.

These groups are helpful for those who are strengthened by companions. The success rate is very high. For example, in one year, three thousand smokers in the Washington, D.C. area faithfully followed this controlled fasting plan. Seven out of every ten succeeded in breaking the smoking habit.

If you fail, don't give up. You haven't lost the war, only a battle. Renew your decision, reiterate your stand, make yourself captain of your destiny.

BENEFITS OF CHEWING

If you feel the need to do something with your mouth in the absence of a cigarette, the 5-Day Plan permits chewing on a prune or an olive and playing with the pit for a while. Chewing gum is also an acceptable antidote for craving for a smoke.

HOW TO CLEANSE YOUR HEART

Ever thought you'd like to houseclean or wash out your heart? This controlled fasting plan can accomplish just that. You see, your heart is a muscle that needs oxygen and food supply. This is transported by the blood in small tubes called arteries. When you smoke, nicotine sends toxic agents to the blood, causes these tubes or blood vessels to constrict, become choked up. When your heart muscle is deprived of blood, it begins to hurt and ache. Further accumulated internal toxic wastes may narrow or stop the blood flow. This leads to an acute coronary-artery heart attack. The controlled fasting plan washes the bloodstream, frees the arteries and blood vessels so they can transport equally clean and fresh nutrients to the heart.

A WONDERFUL FEELING OF HEALTH

No more smoker's throat. No chronic bronchial cough. No more palpitation. Controlled fasting gives a steady heart beat, a calm purse, a sweet breath, a clean mouth, a relaxed body, a mind in control of itself. What more could you want?

Try this special controlled fasting plan in group therapy or on your own, depending upon your own strength of inner resources. Do not be ashamed to admit that tobacco has enslaved you. Admission is the first step to improvement. Ask the help of others if you need them. Perhaps you can form a special Clinic. Ask at your local Health Department.

Free Yourself From Tobacco Highlights

1. Smoking is not an easy habit to kick. Recognize that fact and muster your will power reserves.
2. A 5-day controlled fasting plan may be followed, based on the famous method devised by special stop smoking clinics.
3. You may follow it by yourself or in group therapy.
4. Controlled fasting helps cleanse your heart and wash out the traces of noxious nicotine. It *can* help you get rid of the tobacco habit.

8

Slim Down or Fill Out
with Controlled Fasting

Too fat, too thin? — try controlled fasting for desired results. When you dispose of waste substances in your system, you can help melt away pounds if you are overweight. If you are a "stringbean" type and eat and eat and eat and still do not fill out, it is possible you are eating the wrong foods! *Metabolism* is the internal process by which food substances are broken up and sent to the billions of your body cells for nourishment. The building up process of healing and repair is known as *anabolism;* the breaking down process which releases energy for body use is known as *catabolism.* Both of these methods are responsible for overall body health, weight gain and loss.

Oxygen is very precious for maintenance of body metabolism and weight normalization. Each body cell must have oxygen. When these billions of tissue cells are clogged up with internal toxic wastes, function is impaired and metabolism goes awry. This creates havoc with normal body weight.

Eating is in your nature. Many chubbies lose precious health, let youth and stamina slip through their fingers, maintaining that eating is part of their nature. They just can't help themselves. In a way, this may be true. That is why controlled fasting permits you to eat and achieve a normal weight. Eating *is* your nature and your instinct, too. Sometimes, it can go against your benefit as we see from this old fable about the tortoise and the scorpion.

It seems that the scorpion, a poor swimmer, wanted to cross a river. He asked the turtle if he would allow him to climb on his back so he could get to the other side. "I'd be stupid to do a thing like that," replied the turtle. "You'd sting me and we'd both drown."

"Why should I sting you?" replied the scorpion. "If I did that, we'd both perish. It's completely illogical."

The turtle thought about this for a moment and then agreed, "Okay, hop on."

In the middle of the stream, the scorpion stung the turtle. As they both descended to a watery grave, the turtle gasped, "But you said it would be completely illogical for you to sting me."

"Logic has nothing to do with it," gurgled back the scorpion. "It's just my nature."

You chubbies are in the same situation. You eat and eat and eat, knowing it is illogical and reponsible for ill health, but you continue right on, unable to control yourself, filling your insides with accumulated debris and waste substances because it is just your nature!

WHY OVERWEIGHT IS UNHEALTHY

Numerous ailments are traced to overweight. These include heart disorder, blood vessel damage, degeneration of body tissues caused by waste substances lodged in tissue pockets, diabetic conditions, gall bladder disease, to name just a few.

For example, for each 20 excess pounds, 12 extra miles of blood vessels are needed to pump blood through to the body. The heart must increase its burden and may eventually contribute to a heart attack. As for blood pressure, this represents the *force* of the heart beat. Excess fat is riddled and soaked with toxic wastes that increase the force, raising the pressure level. The kidneys then must work harder to eliminate these toxic waste products and effectiveness may be injured by overwork.

ACCUMULATED WASTES DOWNGRADE THE BODY

The accumulation of waste products and toxic substances downgrade body health. These wastes produce a distortion of the line of gravity of the spine when the stomach becomes heavy and laden. The spine must be pulled forward. This produces a weakness in the vertebrae joints and between the spine and pelvis. Sciatica, a pain radiation down the back of the leg in the sciatic nerve path, may be caused. This is traced to accumulation of waste substances and pressure in the sacroiliac region, the joint between the spine and hipbone. The body breakdown is slow, gradual and insidious. Waste substances cling to one another and grow in accumulation. Health slowly declines while body weight climbs.

"Slow eating will melt your pounds." At 44, Grace was plump (not pleasing because overweight is anything but pleasing), with signs of premature aging, unsightly bulges, pudgy arms and legs. "My husband told me to get out of the house and go to work; anything to keep me out of the kitchen. I just can't stop eating," she complained when she appeared in my New York City office, asking for a job as a bookkeeper. "Maybe it'll keep my mind off food."

We chatted for a while. Before I told her I did not need a bookkeeper, I said that I could help her lose her unsightly weight. "Slow eating will melt your pounds. Together with controlled fasting, as part of a reducing plan devised by a European physician, you can slim down to a lovely figure."

Grace could not believe it. "Slow eating? Controlled fasting? Do you want me to starve?"

"I didn't say a word about starving," was my reply. "I said controlled fasting — you can eat well, to satisfy your eating nature, and still lose weight. Some foods will have to be eliminated completely but you'll get a satisfaction by eating other substitute foods. And you must eat slowly. Will you follow my plan? I'll write it out for you."

Grace agreed. Afterwards, I told her to come back in just fourteen days and we would talk about a bookkeeping job that would keep her out of the kitchen — *if* she found she was still addicted to the munching and nibbling and excessive eating habit.

She did come back — in fourteen days — and looked so slim, it was unbelievable. "Forget about the job, Mr. Wade. I don't want it now. I don't need it. Your plan helped control my appetite. I never knew controlled fasting and slow eating could melt my pounds."

THE SECRET OF SLIMMING DOWN

This method of slimming down is based upon the discovery that liberated enzymes from foods well masticated will help clean out accumulated waste products and restore normal body metabolism. It is based upon a principle advanced by Heinz Humplik, M.D. as reported in the European medical journal, *Munchener Medizinische Wochenschrift* (28:183-86). Here's how it works, and controlled fasting stimulates its efficiency.

Digestion needs energy which is supplied by the burning of calories. The body must work hard to prepare food for absorption. The enzymes work hard to clean out your clogged up food tube and digestive system, ridding your insides of internal poisons and toxic waste accumulations. Slow eating or thorough chewing will release enzymes from masticated foods. If you bolt your food, you tend to eat more, and it remains lodged in your digestive tract, releasing toxic wastes that cling to delicate food tubes and internal organs.

Now, once the thoroughly chewed food is swallowed, enzymes work to make your esophagus contract repeatedly and strenuously to push this food into your stomach. All the while, enzymes are washing your digestive organs. Once your food is in your stomach — rhythmic segmentations and pendulum motions in the small intestines mix the food 1000 times or more, utilizing much internal energy. This action continues to wash out these organs.

The peristaltic waves, muscular contractions that coax food through the intestines and the walls of the long intestine that knead its contents again and again to absorb the nutrients are in ceaseless, calorie-consuming movement during the digestive process. At the same time, enzymes are washing out accumulated wastes that act like magnets and draw substances to add surplus weight.

Therefore, according to Dr. Humplik, you should eat those foods that make your body do more work to burn up more internal calories and also help slough off accumulated toxic wastes in the operation. This is a form of controlled fasting that lets you eat (slow eating, slow and thorough chewing, remember!) and melt pounds, at the same time.

CALORIC PRINCIPLE

"If the body gets 10 calories and needs 11 for utilization," says Dr. Humplik, "then the missing calorie must be supplied by the store that is the adipose (fatty) tissue. The same way, when the body gets 4,000 calories but needs 4,400 for their utilization, then the missing 400 will be taken from the adipose tissue. From all these facts, the therapy for obesity evolves: the more the overweight person eats — controlled fasting by diet — the more he loses weight."

WHAT YOU MAY EAT:

Controlled fasting and internal cleansing to reduce weight lets you eat these foods — lean meat, fowl and hard-boiled eggs; all leafy and root vegetables, plus cucumbers, tomatoes, asparagus, mushrooms and salads; fresh fruits (but *not* bananas, dates, figs and seedless grapes) should be eaten raw and unpeeled, when possible. *NO* carbohydrate foods such as potatoes, bread, macaroni, rice, spaghetti and cereals. (Whatever carbohydrates are needed by your body are contained in raw vegetables, salads and fruits.) Your fats come to you from vegetable oils, that is, unsaturated fatty acids.

WHAT YOU MAY NOT EAT:

These foods not only provide excess calories but leave ash-acid residues that cause internal toxemia. You should *not* eat any of these foods: flour and cereal products, bread, puddings, breaded meat and noodles; no sugar products, including sugar-containing desserts, chocolates, candy, ice cream, honey, marmalade, sugar drinks, pies, and cakes. Omit milk and milk products, omit animal fats, alcohol and coffee.

How to Satisfy "That" Urge. To satisfy your urge for sweets, try the dietetic desserts and foods made without sugar. Most food outlets have special sections selling such foods. Look in your local health food shop, too.

SPECIAL INTERNAL CLEANSING DIET

Dr. Humplik recommends a three-day controlled fasting plan designed to melt pounds and clean out accumulated toxic wastes. This can be summarized as follows:

FIRST DAY:

Breakfast — Choose large quantities of either lean tongue, roast beef, cold boiled beef, two or three hard boiled eggs. Choose between raw sauerkraut, radishes, raw cucumbers, paprika sprouts (green) and any kind of herb tea such as peppermint, rose hips, camomile, fenugreek — but no coffee or commercial tea.

Luncheon — Eat oranges or unpeeled apples or pears.

Dinner — Begin with a hardy supply of green salad (five times normal portion with salad dressing of vegetable oil and apple cider vinegar), at least 8 ounces of boiled beef, dessert of a raw vegetable salad. After that, only herb tea.

SECOND DAY:

Throughout this day, eat as much as possible of fresh raw fruits at one meal; then eat fresh raw vegetables at another meal such as radishes, celery, fresh cucumbers, paprika sprouts and tomatoes. Do not use any vegetable oil on this second day. Throughout the day, whenever the urge to eat comes upon you, prepare either a fruit dish or a vegetable dish and that is to be your meal. Eat as much as you want!

THIRD DAY:

Repeat first day's menu with this addition — fresh raw fruit every two hours, in between meals.

This 3-day controlled fasting plan will help cleanse your insides to the point where pounds will melt away. Also, remember to eat slowly and chew slowly when you partake of your meals, as this liberates digestive and internal cleansing enzymes that sweep out your insides and wash out your digestive apparatus.

At the end of your three day period, go back to your usual diet — but you keep in practice the foods that you may eat and may *not* eat. That is, if you want to keep slimming down and want to maintain normal weight, refrain from the foods that you may *not* eat, and substitute with lots of fresh fruit or dietetic sweets that are sugar and carbohydrate-free.

WHAT ABOUT WATER AND SALT?

Those experienced in *fastology* — the theory about washing out insides and controlled eating — have found that water helps wash out the insides but only slows up digestive processes if you drink it during meals. So do not drink water *with* meals. Drink two hours before or after meals.

As for salt, this introduces an acid-ash into the system, clogging up the internal organs, impeding digestive processes, too. Some people retain the water they drink with the salt used in food. The water and salt stay in body tissues, creating an unhealthy condition of internal toxemia. Eliminate salt from your meals and give your recuperative processes a chance to go to work to self-cleanse out your insides. Use salt substitutes that have a vegetarian basis. Ask at any diet counter or health store for these non-salt flavoring agents.

HOW TO GAIN WEIGHT BY CONTROLLED FASTING

It's no joke being called "skinny" or "beanpole." I know how it feels to be thusly hurt because I was always called by such unflattering names. When I was a teen-ager, I was six feet, three inches tall and a wiry 144 pounds! I was thin as a rail. I thought I could gain weight by stuffing myself, but gobs of sweets and starches set up a turbulent internal toxic revolution — waste substances accumulated, tried to get out by giving me a bad case of pimples and dandruff, made me perspire all the time, caused unsightly boils and facial and body blemishes.

Nature wanted to get rid of these toxic wastes that were hindering digestive powers, interfering with caloric function, preventing normal weight gains. My insides were clogged up with the residue and wastes that adhered to my digestive organs.

I endured these taunts, became a shy wallflower, developed a serious inferiority complex. Who wouldn't feel inferior at six feet, three inches tall, at the age of 17, with pimples, blackheads, acne, dandruff all over the body and a bony, skinny body at that, too!

"Wash out your insides!" That nugget of advice was given to me by an old-fashioned family doctor, the type that is slowly vanishing from our scene. "You can't achieve a normal weight with dirty insides. Certain foods cause a collection of internal bacteria at a point where it multiplies, produces toxins which are absorbed by your bloodstream and spreads throughout your body. These toxins want to get out but can't because you keep eating more and more wrong foods. The toxic wastes try to escape through skin pores and . . . well, a look in the mirror at your face will prove that."

"How can I clean out my insides?" was my wailing plea.

"Controlled fasting — you have to increase intake of certain foods, reduce and eliminate other foods. You drink all you want of freshly squeezed fruit and vegetable juices — not together, but at separate intervals — but you omit waste-forming foods."

TOXIN-CAUSING FOODS

In my particular situation, these toxin-causing foods were eliminated from my diet: biscuits and crackers, bread and rolls, cakes, candied fruits, candy, cereals, condensed milk, doughnuts, canned or fancy fruits, dried fruits, jam and jelly, marmalades, marshallow, milk chocolate, popcorn, sugars and syrups and foods containing those sweetenings.

I followed my kindly doctor's advice but continued eating other foods such as lean meats, poultry, fish, etc. Within four weeks, my complexion began to clear up and become blemish-free (it still has that youthful fresh-as-a-rose look), I put on healthy pounds, began to fill out. With my change of appearance, my personality emerged from its shell, I became more popular and was much sought after for social affairs, dances and dates. I became a new person by this controlled fasting plan that let me fill out and clean out, at the same time. All this was accomplished by elimination of those foods that cause internal waste residues.

Today, I still follow this rigid controlled fasting plan and feel fit as the proverbial fiddle. I fervently hope that others will benefit, too.

Yes, eating *is* your nature. Make it a wonderful, joyful experience by eating the right foods that will satisfy and self-cleanse at the same time.

You may rightfully insist that you're still hungry. Then you must be "cheating" and eating the taboo foods. These aforementioned taboo foods create a toxic whiplash in your system that stimulate appetite. Remove them, cleanse your insides and control your appetite. Eating can be fun — when it builds your health. Not when it destroys it!

Slenderizing Tips in Chapter 8

1. Overweight is related to accumulated waste products in your system.
2. Chew long to let your insides work and thereby cleanse toxic wastes while expending fat-forming calories.
3. Follow special controlled fasting methods to gain weight. Be cautious about salt, water. Learn which foods to eat, which to avoid.

9

How to Achieve Superior Brain Power with Controlled Fasting

The famous writer-explorer, Rex Beach, who once mined gold in Alaska, wrote of gold miners: "We ate greatly of baking-powder bread, underdone beans and fat pork. No sooner were these victuals down than they went to war on us. The real call of the wild was not the howl of the timber wolf, the maniac laughter of the Arctic loon, or the mating cry of the bull moose; it was the dyspeptic belch of the miner!"

Improper eating had completely altered the mental stamina of these gold miners, wrongly affecting brain power. Internal toxins had created gastro-intestinal decomposition and distress that was carried via the bloodstream and respiratory systems to the brain, drenching the delicate tissues of the brain, creating mental havoc. Bacterial decomposition and fermentation upset the balance of the delicate mental and nervous systems.

LET'S LOOK AT YOUR BRAIN

The ancient Greeks (who practiced controlled fasting and were reputed to be the healthiest people in the then-known world) believed that the epitome of life is to have a healthy mind in a healthy body. This is possible when you have a *clean mind or brain in an internally cleansed body*. Let's see how this is possible.

Your brain is the most essential portion of your nervous system. It consists of about 16 billion cells and tissues that must be clean, fresh and vigorous. The brain is made up of 3 main parts — the frontal part (cerebrum), the hind part (cerebellum), and the medulla oblongata by which it is connected to the spinal cord and therefore, to all body nerves.

The average man's brain weighs about 48 ounces. A woman's brain weighs slightly less, but relative to body weight, there is little difference. Truthfully, though, more intelligent people have been noted to possess heavier brains — but brains weighing as much as 62 ounces have been found in idiots. Normal intelligence depends upon a clean brain that weighs a minimum of 32 ounces, however.

POWER OF YOUR BRAIN

No single body movement is possible without the cooperation of your brain. You want to turn a page in this book. The very thought sends a nerve impulse to your brain. That is, an electrical current moves along a specific path to a certain segment of your brain that then provides the power to lift your hand to turn this page.

Within your brain are special centers that control all you do or feel. There is, for instance, the respiratory center to control your breathing. There is the olfactory center that lets you smell, the auditory center that lets you hear, the visual center that lets you see, the taste center that lets you taste. You have other centers that let you speak, enjoy and create music, perform writing and reading. You have a motor center in your brain that decides your body motions.

Here, in your brain, you have a fascinating vaso-constrictor center that contracts your blood vessel walls. You have a center that controls chewing, swallowing, coughing, sneezing, eye blinking, etc. A certain center in your brain influences the secretion of stomach juices, the intestinal movements.

Your brain has what is called autonomic — or automatic — powers. Your brain lets you breathe and blink throughout the day and night, although you are rarely aware of these functions. In fact, your brain is so powerful, it rules some of your emotions without your control. If you are suddenly embarrassed or ashamed, the vaso-constrictor center of your brain is temporarily shut off by this emotion, causing your facial blood vessels to become dilated with blood. This is known as a "reflex" action; that is, it occurs without your consent or conscious knowledge and there is nothing you can do to interfere. If you doubt the all-power of your brain, try to learn how not to blush. It's impossible. Surrender to your brain power.

Intelligence, mental health, superior intellect, mind power, all come from *a healthy and detoxified brain.* That is, the brain must have clean and healthy tissues — all 16 billion cells should be free of toxic wastes and accumulated sludge products.

HOW A CHRONIC ABSENTEE PROBLEM WAS SOLVED

A small manufacturer who believed in treating employees fairly decided to put in a small company-sponsored cafeteria. This would eliminate time lost in driving to nearby restaurants for lunches or occasional snacks.

He served adequate (sometimes *too* adequate) meals to his employees. "I hoped this would make them feel better, work better, especially since my production rate was on the increase and there were deadlines to meet. Instead, many of the workers had to go to the company lounge and take frequent naps. Some could hardly keep their eyes open," was his complaint. "In fact, my secretary made so many mistakes when taking my dictation, I thought something was wrong with her. What's the problem?"

I was paying him a social call, preparatory to researching an article assignment given me by a large magazine publisher on efficiency in the factory. "Let's go to your cafeteria and see how they eat," was my suggestion. It was lunch time.

We got in line with the employees and moved along the counter. That was when I noticed something unusual. "Don't you give them specified portions?"

The manufacturer shook his head. "No. It saves time to have full meals prepared and given out, rather than individual selections. No substitutions or else they'd be changing the menu. Too confusing."

The employees ate heartily and heavily. The foods ladled out were heavy in starch and carbohydrates as well as sweets. Many of the employees had to open belts during the lunch. Many looked sleepy while eating at the table.

"That's your problem," I explained to the manufacturer. "You're giving them heavy carbohydrate food. It's dulling their senses. I suggest you cut down the portions, substitute more fresh fruits and vegetables. Use smaller plates to create an illusion of quantity. See how that works."

It *did* work. The employees were not so fatigued as before, cut down the sneaky trips to the lounge to lie down, felt more alert. Some employees resigned because they had become accustomed to those hearty free lunches and felt cheated. I told the manufacturer that he was better off without an employee who had a "sluggish brain."

That is precisely what occurred. The chronic work absentee problem could be traced to the illness of a sluggish brain.

EFFECT OF TOXEMIA-DRENCHED BRAIN CELLS

The 16 billion brain cells, like the many billions of body brain cells, have to be kept clean, washed and sparkling. These brain cells do need oxygen and food. Your blood carries oxygen and food to these brain cells via four essential arteries. When oxygen and food are laden with deposits, waste substances, toxic elements, the brain cells become drenched with these sludge substances, tend to become clogged. Efficiency is obviously impeded.

A full stomach does not like to think! So spoke the ancients. The process of digestion also draws away so much oxygen and blood from other body parts, the brain is deprived of its just supplies and it grows weak. That explains the feeling of drowsiness and sleepiness, following a heavy meal. It also explains why so many employees and average folk feel inefficient after a heavy noon meal. The brain becomes starved for blood and oxygen that is being rerouted to the digestive organs. Later, when blood and oxygen bearing nutrients are sent back to the brain, these elements are saturated with waste substances;that clog up the delicate brain cells.

We can see a noticeable deterioration in mental energies among our young who gobble down cola drinks, hot dogs, ice cream, candies, etc. These foods send toxic wastes to the brain via the bloodstream and create an unhealthy chain reaction of internal toxemia.

It is estimated that some 20 million Americans have nervous or mental disorders that are serious enough to warrant treatment.

TOXIN-FORMING FOODS

Because brain cells are super-sensitive to disturbances and react sharply to the influence of toxic waste residues, certain foods should be decreased and eliminated from the diet. This form of controlled fasting will help cleanse and wash your bloodstream and provide healthy oxygen to the brain.

1. *Bleached white flour foods.* In his syndicated column, William Brady, M.D., wrote that "dogs fed mainly on entirely white bread or white flour products may develop what is mistaken for rabies — shunning food, losing weight, avoiding light, trembling, cringing when patted, climbing walls, falling backwards, howling piteously, falling into their pans if they try to eat, and running around madly." Apparently, the chemicalized white flour foods saturate the brain cells with toxic residues that completely alter the health of the mental pattern.

2. *Coffee and tea.* Caffeine and tannic acids are narcotics that whip up the blood sugar level, cause a severe up-and-down yank until the mind is a whirl. Substitute, instead, caffeine-free coffee and herb teas sold at most diet shoppes or health food stores.

3. *Soft drinks.* Again, certain narcotics are present in bottled or tap soft drinks that infiltrate the bloodstream and may corrode delicate body tissues and that includes the tissues of the brain. Drink fresh fruit and vegetable drinks.

4. *Prepared meats.* This includes corned beef, frankfurters, bologna, salami, sausages, etc. All are saturated with preservatives, chemicals, artificial dyes, inks, paints, etc. They become transformed into toxic wastes and exert harmful influences upon the brain and body cells.

5. *Candy and cake.* Again we face the problem of artificial colorings and flavorings as well as chemical additives that are unnatural and unacceptable to the body. This includes pies, jellies, jams, marmalades, baked goods, canned desserts, etc. Substitute with natural desserts. A fresh apple or a dish of diced pineapple is delicious and healthy and toxic-free.

Select unprocessed foods and those that are as natural as possible.

BRAIN-CLEANSING CONTROLLED FASTING PLAN

According to Sam E. Roberts, M.D., brain or mental disorders may be relieved by controlled dietary methods. You may be able to perk up mental vigor, enjoy tremendous mental power and increased intelligence with a healthy and tissue-cleansed brain. Dr. Roberts who is also an allergist-specialist, states, "All age-groups are subject to metabolic dysfunctions, even the allergic-asthmatic child ... The symptoms are mostly bizarre and stimulate a neurosis, at times even a psychosis ... It may also be the precursor (forerunner) for many pathologic conditions which are today of unknown etiology (cause) ... It is the enigma that prompts most patients to report to physicians or to clinics, for a complete checkup because of 'utter exhaustion.'"

Dr. Roberts believes a patient should be given a special blood test to see if there are any disorders. Mental disorders among his own patients included nervous habits such as fingernail biting, bed wetting, depression, insomnia. There were symptoms of tightness in the chest and pain in various body parts, migraine, deafness, nasal allergy, constant hunger, eyeache, and swollen feet.

Based upon his findings, here is a special controlled fasting plan to help those who want to enjoy superior brain power:

1. Eliminate cigarettes, alcohol, and coffee.
2. Eliminate all sugars and starches.
3. Bread should be a whole grain type and should consist of no more than two very thin slices daily.
4. For a morning eye-opener, eat a piece of raw fruit (such as banana) *before* your breakfast. This helps start the internal cleansing action. Your breakfast should be high-protein — fruit, eggs and meat or both but *no* starches as these create ash residue and clutter bloodstream. Your lunch should have a glass of tomato juice with a teaspoon of brewer's yeast and a teaspoon of wheat germ (sold at health stores). Dr. Roberts adds lemon juice and rind. Then, have fish with salad, hard boiled egg. Lunch dessert is fresh, raw fruit. Your dinner should be a high protein dish such as meat or poultry, together with lots of fresh, raw vegetables.

Prune juices and grapes are not recommended because they are rich in sugar which may upset the blood sugar level. Avoid gravies or sauces that are made with flour. Do *not* add sugar to anything. Refined white sugar introduces much toxic wastes and residues into the bloodstream which is then carried to the brain cells.

FIGS: ANCIENT BRAIN FOOD

The ancients who displayed superior intelligence were often great fig eaters. It was Pliny, the Roman naturalist of the first century, A.D., who wrote:

"Figs are restorative, and the best food that can be taken by those who are brought low by long sickness, and are on the way to recovery. They increase the mental strength of young people, preserve the elderly in better mind health and make them look younger, and with fewer wrinkles. They are so nutritive as to cause strength; for this cause, professed wrestlers and champions were in times past fed with figs."

Figs were used by some people as their exclusive diet. They were probably first raised in South Arabia; were known to the Greeks back in the 9th century, B.C. An Egyptian papyrus dated 1552 B.C. mentions that figs were used by scribes and philosophers. Many scholars of ancient days would fast for days, eating figs and drinking fresh water. It was said that superior mental power could be traced to figs.

How figs work. There is a peculiar substance in the seeds of figs that exert a cleansing action upon the bloodstream. Figs have a precious enzyme called *ficin* or *cradein* which are empowered to engulf and dissolve toxic elements in the bloodstream, purifying this precious internal river of life. Other as yet unidentified ingredients make the fig a superior food — try eating figs to cleanse the bloodstream and help improve mental power. Select organically grown figs. Munch them for snacks or desserts. Eat the *whole* fresh fig because its seeds — those tiny, crunchy specks — are said to have certain ingredients that nourish the billions of brain cells. Chew them carefully to get all possible benefit from fig seeds.

You have only one brain! Treat it well and you'll be rewarded with a healthy mind and a healthy body.

What You Discovered in this Chapter

1. Your brain has some 16 million cells and tissues that must be fed with a clean and toxic-free bloodstream and fresh oxygen supply.
2. All body functions depend upon a healthy brain.
3. A full stomach drains brain power. Try eating smaller meals prior to heavy thinking sessions.
4. Avoid the toxic-forming foods that include bleached white flour products, coffee and tea, soft drinks, prepared meats, candy and cakes. Substitute natural, unprocessed and organic foods.
5. Try the special brain cleansing, controlled fasting plan designed to improve and strengthen your mental powers.
6. Figs were used by ancients to stimulate brain power.

10

How Controlled Fasting Oils Your Arteries for Health

You are as young as your arteries! This network running through your entire body from head to toe is charged with the responsibility of transporting nutrient-carrying blood and oxygen to all of your valuable organs. Like any wire network, the arterial structure must be kept well lubricated and in smooth working order if you want to enjoy the best of life, health and youth.

As stated earlier, your body is a waste-forming biochemical entity. That is, ingested foods leave an accumulation of toxic substances that cling to most of your internal organs and particularly your arteries. Just as any pipe, wire, or coil springs must be periodically cleansed, so must your arteries be oiled and cleansed of accumulated clinging wastes. This is where controlled fasting comes into being.

Your arteries are your lifelines of health. Clean, lubricated and well-oiled arteries can function properly. Encrusted, dirt-clogged arteries lose efficiency and health starts a slow slipping, bit by bit. Because arterial difficulties are associated with middle-age, it is obvious that years and years of internal toxemia have taken their toll. Many authorities agree that life begins at 40 — but with the vibrant health of 20! It's wonderful to reach the age of 40 — if you feel like 20! That is where your arteries come in.

WHAT ARE ARTERIES?

The arteries are the elastic tubes through which nutrient-carrying blood, reinforced with precious oxygen, is transported from your heart to all body parts. The arteries are elastic in that they can contract or expand as the heartbeat forces more or less blood into them.

Arterial blood is always under pressure, similar to air inside a balloon. The ancients assumed that the arteries exist solely for the purpose of transporting oxygen and named them *arteries* which is derived from the Latin word meaning "windpipe." They do transport oxygen, but also blood, as well.

The main artery of your heart is the *aorta,* about one inch wide or so, at the portion where it leaves the heart's left section. The aorta branches out into smaller arteries which transport blood to your head, stomach, arms, legs, etc. The arterial network becomes a tremendous system of large and small arteries that extend in all directions, carrying blood with its oxygen and other nutrient substances to just about every single tissue and cell in your body. The large arteries subdivide first into smaller arteries, then into still smaller arteries, finally into the minute, hairlike blood vessels known as *capillaries.*

WHAT ARE CAPILLARIES?

These are minute, thin-walled hairlike channels that end to end would stretch for thousands of miles; they reach into every crevice and nook in your body; they transport food and oxygen to all body cells and remove the accumulation of toxic wastes and internal refuse products.

Simultaneously, at countless different sites in your body, this interchange between capillaries and tissue cells takes place through the very thin capillary wall.

This interchange process, termed *osmosis,* is comparable to the exchange transportation of two liquids that are divided by a thin, permeable or porous membrane. In your body, this process of osmosis — internal housecleaning — takes place by which the cells take the oxygen and other precious nutrients from your blood and surrender their waste substances. *Note carefully* — healthy arteries will enable your cells to perform osmosis and get rid of toxemia. Otherwise, these wastes accumulate and create a situation of unclean insides.

As Fritz Kahn, M.D., in *Man In Structure And Function,* once remarked, each capillary is "fifty times finer than the finest human hair," and is so minute that about 700 capillaries could be packed into the space occupied by the thickness of a pin!

Through these microscopic blood vessels, your blood corpuscles march in single file, carrying nutritive substances and oxygen to the cells — but must also take away their toxins. Any residue left will remain in the arterial structure, clogging up efficiency like rust or slime, or chalk.

So we see that the capillaries — smallest arterial subdivision — also form the start of the veins. Related capillaries combine to form small veins, *venulea,* from which (by means of fusion) larger veins come into being.

WHAT ARE VEINS?

Derived from the Latin word *vena* which means "blood vessel," in a loose interpretation, your veins transport the oxygen-drained and poison and toxin filled blood back to the right side of the heart. Here, this blood is pumped into the lungs to be purified and re-oxygenated.

The arteries, by the way, are closer to the pumping heart, vulnerable to its full force and have a much heavier load to carry. Both arteries and veins belong to the circulatory system, but the arteries are more powerfully developed and have more resiliency than the veins.

But the veins have another protective feature. They are covered with valves to prevent the blood from flowing back. The veins are further away from the heart, derive less of its pumping force, so must have its own built-in protection. These valves must also be kept clean, lubricated and in good working order.

WHY YOU MUST KEEP BLOOD CHANNELS CLEAN

You can readily see how internal toxemia, waste accumulations and poisonous substances that are not swept up by the process of osmosis and remain in sticky adhesion to the cells, arteries, capillaries, veins, etc., can create a health hazard condition. This is a serious condition because your life depends upon clean and young and resilient arteries. Toxemia-filled arteries can cause heart attacks and serious blood vessel disorders.

It is estimated that every two minutes — the time it takes you to read this page — someone will die of heart disease. In fact, the leading death cause in this country is traced to heart and blood vessel diseases. (Twice the death rate of cancer.) Clogged arteries are responsible for more deaths below the age of 65 than five other major causes! So you can readily appreciate the necessity for keeping your arteries clean and well oiled. Especially when it is said that close to 800,000 deaths in one year are traced to arterial disease.

THE CONSEQUENCES OF DIRTY ARTERIES

It sounds unpleasant to say that you may have dirty arteries but it's far more unpleasant to cheat precious years from your life because of this condition. These are the two serious conditions of unclean and toxemia-infected arteries:

1. *Atherosclerosis* (*ather* is from the Greek *athere,* "mush" or "porridge," to describe deposits in the arteries, plus *sclerosis,* meaning "hardening" results from the depositing of cholesterol in the arteries.) Deposits of this fatty-like substance will thicken and harden the arteries.
2. *Arteriosclerosis* (*arterio* is from the Greek, arteries, plus *sclerosis,* or "hardening.") That is, the arteries, themselves, become hardened.

Both of these conditions are deliberately traced to unclean and waste-infested arteries that become clogged with slime and sludge.

WHAT IS CHOLESTEROL?

The word originates from the Greek, *chole* for "bile" and *sterol,* also from the Greek, meaning "solid." That is exactly what cholesterol is: a fatty substance found first in the digestive bile and then elsewhere; it is also the stuff of which some gallstones are composed. The Merck Index says of cholesterol that it is "the principal sterol of the higher animals (meaning we humans), found in all body tissues."

Back in 1814, a French chemist, Michel Eugene Chevreul, discovered this substance. Early researchers did not know how serious it could be but in 1872, the brilliant English physiologist, Thomas Huxley, described it as "a remarkable crystalline substance, very fatty looking, but not really of a fatty nature." He hinted vaguely that it could clog up the system and impair health. Thus, internal toxemia and cholesterol were related.

In 1913, Nikolai Nikolaievich Anichkov fed test animals on a high-cholesterol diet and saw that they developed dirty arteries — he called them arterial plaques — which hampered the function of these valuable wire networks.

In years to come, others found that unclean arteries that were covered with cholesterol — actually, waste products and toxic poisons — could seriously deplete health.

A CLOSE LOOK AT ARTERIAL-TOXEMIA

Closer examination of arteries will show *atheromas* — that is, masses of mushy yellowish material just under the artery lining. These masses bulge into the channel, may eventually obstruct it completely. Atheromas usually start as collection of toxemia-drenched cells that have cholesterol. Arterial-toxemia is readily identified as being bubbly and foamy. If the arteries are not cleansed through a proper controlled fasting plan, then the cells containing the cholesterol die, release it into the artery lining where it crystalizes.

Crystalline cholesterol is an irritant; it causes an increase in the fibrous structure of the artery lining, building up a heavy layer or plaque of fibrous substance. This fibrous area may eventually calcify and turn to stone-hard material. Thus, the condition of hardening of the arteries is begun.

THE SERIOUS THREAT TO YOUR HEART

Arterial-toxemia's most serious threat is that the artery will narrow to the point where the blood flow is obstructed and a clot forms. A clot is called a *thrombus,* the condition is known as thrombosis — a heart attack! More advanced symptoms of arterial-toxemia include obstructed arteries that may burst. How? A stiff, brittle artery becomes kinked because of the accumulated sludge and slime; a high-pressure surge of blood is forced through, actually rupturing the artery!

WHERE DOES ARTERIAL-TOXEMIA STRIKE?

Danger spots are these:
1. The aorta. While large enough to adapt to partial channel clogging, the wall of this artery may weaken, bulge and perhaps burst.
2. The legs. Obstruction of toxic wastes may cause tissue death; symptoms often start as tingling or cramps, aches or sharp pains when you use your legs.
3. The brain. Here, toxic-drenched arteries may burst, leading to death of brain tissue. This is known as *apoplexy* or a stroke!
4. The heart. Called coronary occlusion (closure) of a coronary artery. A toxemia-infested artery deprives the heart muscle of blood and oxygen. The heart becomes so "starved," it grows weak, it quivers instead of beats. This is called *fibrillation* — toxemia has choked off the food supply to the heart so it cannot pump well.

More serious ailments may be these:
A. A portion of the heart muscle becomes *necrotic* — dead; if it is a large portion, the heart succumbs to toxemia in a few days and life is snuffed out.
B. The heart lining over this toxemia-infected area may become the site of a blood clot (called a *mural thrombus* because the toxic wastes are fettered to the heart wall). If portions of such a clot break loose and float away, they create debris-ridden conditions that obstruct important arteries.

C. The toxemia-drenched portion of the heart muscle may become healed, so to speak, turning into a dense scar. A scar is an impediment to the pumping heart and drags on its activities. In later years, heart failure may occur.

WHAT CAUSES TOXIC WASTES IN THE BLOOD STREAM

Before we go into the foods that are responsible for formation of toxemia and cholesterol, and a special artery-oiling and artery-washing program, let's see some other causative factors:

1. *High blood pressure* encourages accumulation of arterial cholesterol and toxemia in your arteries.
2. *High blood cholesterol* is responsible for toxic deposits. Diabetics, for instance, are known for having more than normal toxic cholesterol.
3. *Overweight* people have more waste substances in their blood and excessive cholesterol.

    Preceding chapters in this volume pointed out how debris-filled blood can cause accumulation of toxemia and poisonous substances that are related to conditions of high blood pressure, overweight, etc. Re-read them to see how controlled fasting may help nip this problem in the bud.
4. *Cholesterol in foods* leave ash residues that must be cleansed from the arterial network to keep them in supple condition.

CONTROLLED FASTING IS THE KEY TO CLEANSING ARTERIES

Overeating and excessive eating loads the body up with toxic waste substances ... especially when you eat the wrong foods. Controlled fasting is the key to oiling and washing your arteries.

According to Carrol S. Small, M.D. *(Life And Health* (Vol 73, No. 3), "How can just eating too much food in general raise the blood cholesterol? All the food substances in the body converge during their assimilation at one chemical crossroads. From this crossroads the parts, reassembled in new forms, may emerge as either protein, fat, carbohydrate or cholesterol. Consequently, if a person eats largely of starches and sugars — more than his daily activity and need for warmth demand — he will use the excess to make fat, and may use some to make cholesterol."

Dr. Small adds that the amount of cholesterol in the diet is secondary to the amount of toxic wastes in the blood!

Since food cholesterol is found basically in hard fat and milk products, animal fat sources, etc., perhaps we may recall this gem of wisdom — God gave to Moses as part of the Israelite health code the rule, "It shall be a perpetual statute for your generations throughout all your dwellings that ye eat neither fat nor blood." (Leviticus 3:17). Of course, no one should eliminate fats from the diet since certain vitamins such as A, D, and K as well as other nutrients are assimilated by fat. *The trick is to reduce animal fat sources*. More about this very shortly.

TOBACCO IS A DEBRIS-DIRT SOURCE

Cigarette smoking can increase the levels of circulating free fatty acids and in turn, blood cholesterol, according to a group of Philadelphia General Hospital researchers. Heading the committee, Dr. Alfred Kershbaum found that serum free fatty acid rose 350 milli-equivalents per quart in 17 subjects after they smoked two cigarettes within ten minutes. The elevations remained for 40 minutes after smoking; if the subject was a chain smoker, high cholesterol levels lasted for more than an hour.

Nicotine, the doctors believe, acts as a stimulus to the adrenals to secrete *epinephrine* — a substance that mobilizes the fatty acids from the fat stores and produces a rise in plasma (blood) cholesterol.

They conclude by suggesting that smoking may be a factor in the production of atherosclerosis by the elevation of blood-circulating lipids and alterations in lipid metabolism. Obviously, smoking introduces toxic wastes and poisons that whip up cholesterol and spread it to all body parts. Read Chapter 7 to find out how to end the smoking habit by a 5-day plan of controlled fasting.

NORMAL FUNCTION OF CHOLESTEROL.

Cholesterol is a normal and essential constituent of blood, nerve tissue and other body parts. Normally, it is manufactured in all body cells, especially in your liver. Chiefly, it is formed from *saturated fats* found in certain foods. Cholesterol is deposited along the arterial walls, exerting a toxemia or poisoned condition by dirtying these wires; they become encrusted and so thick and hard they strangle these essential blood network systems.

How can you wash off this dirty slough? To begin, heed the advice of the American Heart Association, "The reduction or *control of fat consumption* under medical supervision, with reasonable substitution of polyunsaturated for saturated fats, is recommended as a possible means preventing atherosclerosis and decreasing the risk of heart attacks and strokes."

THE THREE TYPES OF FATS YOU SHOULD KNOW ABOUT

Controlled fasting begins with the reduction and substitution of foods that contain saturated (hard) fats that leave a toxic waste residue that may accumulate in the bloodstream. Consult this following chart and see which foods are to be reduced, which are to be increased.

1. SATURATED FATS

These tend to form cholesterol. Foods to be reduced in intake because they have a high rate of ash residue, include beef, veal, lamb, pork (best to eliminate pork entirely), hydrogenated shortenings (solid form), chocolate, coconut, ice cream, butter, whole milk and whole-milk cheeses, cream. Substitute with soya milk products sold in health stores.

2. MONO-UNSATURATED FATS

Will not do much internal cleansing action on accumulated toxic wastes. These foods include olive oil, chicken, turkey, duck, almonds, pecans, peanuts, peanut oil, cashew nuts. Eat these in moderation.

3. POLY-UNSATURATED FATS

It has been seen that these foods are able to lower cholesterol rate, have an *internal cleansing action,* are able to wash out your arteries. Step up your intake of fish, corn oil, sunflower oil, soybean oil, safflower oil, herring oil, salad dressing made with vegetable oil, walnuts. Most food outlets sell these items or, try your health food stores.

NORMAL CHOLESTEROL LEVEL

You do have a need for cholesterol in your body but it must remain a comfortable level. Lester Morrison, M.D., author of *The Low Fat Way To Longer Life,* tells us, "People who are fortunate enough to possess a low-cholesterol level (fixed around a 200 milligram value) are able to handle all fats ingested. They are usually characterized by outstanding vitality and inclined to long lives. They rarely suffer from blood vessel diseases and heart attacks."

A doctor can test your cholesterol level in his office.

At one time, it was felt that internal toxemia related to clogged arteries affected oldsters. Today, with high fat intake, young people succumb to the effects of internal toxemia quite readily. Heart disease is the deadliest killer — almost 1 million yearly, including 50 percent of the men who die between 45 and 65. Also, 1 out of every 10 deaths under the age of 35 is traced to heart disease. The ratio jumps after age 35 to 1 death out of every 3. About 250,000 people yearly die prematurely — before 65 — of some kind of heart disease.

Since your heart health depends upon well-oiled arteries, you can understand how essential it is to wash out these lifelines of health through controlled fasting methods.

UNSATURATED VEGETABLE OILS

It has been seen that vegetable oils have a way of dissolving cholesterol and washing the arteries. Substitute animal-source oils with vegetable oils that include corn oil, cottonseed oil, soybean oil, sunflower seed oil, peanut oil, wheat germ oil, etc. The unsaturated fatty acids in these oils have an internal cleansing and internal washing action in that they free the sludge and mush from the arteries and help transport them to be excreted and given off.

AVOID THESE FOODS

Creamed soups which are high in fat content, sweetbreads, brains, kidneys, caviar, fish roe, giblets, pork and all pork products. Fish to avoid are bass, bluefish, butterfish, deviled crab, eel, herring, oysters, salmon, sardines, trout, shad, mackerel. Duck and goose have high fat content. Avoid cheeses such as American, cheddar, Swiss, cream, Edam, Roquefort. Avoid breads such as sweet rolls, waffles, pancakes, buns, doughnuts, pastries. Avoid cookies, pies, cakes, pastries, custards, eclairs, gingerbread, ice cream frozen creams and parfaits. *Eliminate* frying because this process breaks up fat globules in the food and coats the arteries during the digestive process.

EAT THESE FOODS

All lean meats, lean poultry, low-fat fish, plenty of vegetable oils; emphasize clear bouillons and consomme soups, vegetable broths and soups made from skimmed milk. Eat beef, veal, lamb — *but trim off all visible fat!!!* Meats which bear the stamp U.S. GOOD have less fat. Low-fat fish are perch, haddock, smelts, scallops, flounder, sturgeon. The light part of chicken and turkey is good but throw away the skin. Egg white is good but egg yolk has high cholesterol. Skimmed or non-fat milk is good, and so is buttermilk. Fruits and vegetables are good. Salads should be raw. Salad dressings should be made with vegetable oils. Use whole wheat and whole grain cereals with skim milk and fresh fruit. Whole wheat bread.

SOME ARTERY-WASHING TIPS

According to *Nutrition and Atherosclerosis*, a source book on the subject by Louis N. Katz, M.D., you should avoid saturated fats, fried and deep-fried foods which only clog your arteries if taken to excess. But to wash your arteries, here some tips, based on the book:

1. Dessert should be fruits instead of pie, cake, ice cream or any heavy sweet.
2. Correct weight by eating less fat, less refined sweet and starchy foods, less processed fats, no alcoholic drinks. Use a vegetable fat instead of saturated fat.
3. For breakfast, avoid conventional bacon, fried eggs, buttered toast and creamed coffee. Instead, enjoy a breakfast of fresh fruit, whole-grain cereals, skim milk, whole grain bread.

SWEEP CLEAN WITH ALFALFA SPROUTS

A neighbor woman who had a little country farm told me that she underwent a complete physical examination and was informed by her doctor that she had a high cholesterol blood rate. The doctor said that the normal amount in a person's bloodstream is 250 milligrams per 100 cubic centimeters of blood or less.

My reply was, "But the cholesterol level varies according to so many influences; even tension can raise the cholesterol level."

She nodded. "But he said I had a 400 milligram level. I asked him what to do and he suggested alfalfa sprouts — said it would sweep my arteries clean, brush out the toxic wastes and help oil them. Of course, I reduced my hard fat intake, as well."

This was interesting and I asked her to tell me more about alfalfa sprouts — especially when she said that after two months of eating this natural food, her level of cholesterol dropped down to a safe 200 milligrams. Here is what this neighbor woman said. (I might add that since she had her own little country farm she spent a summer growing her own alfalfa. You can buy these sprouts in health stores.)

Alfalfa is a legume, belonging to the bean and pea family. You may eat the leaves, stems and seeds of this plant. If you can grow it, note that its roots burrow as far down in the soil as 20 feet — some roots go as far down as 125 feet, taking up the precious minerals in the soil.

It grows easily in most soils, requires little care. Follow seed directions on the package. If you buy alfalfa — available as seeds or leaves in health stores — you can eat them with ease. Some stores sell them in tablet form as a food supplement. Alfalfa is a prime source of Vitamin A, B-complex, Vitamin E and especially Vitamin K which helps protect against hemorrhaging and — here is the secret — also helps sweep clean your arteries! If you can go into an alfalfa field, pick some stalks and leaves and chew them for dinner.

(I did this when I visited the neighbor woman's farm and felt just wonderful.)

TO SPROUT SEEDS

Most seed stores have alfalfa seeds. Ask for *live* ones. Take home, wash thoroughly, eliminate the cracked and broken seeds. Put in a jug. Cover them with three times the amount of seeds with warm water (about 75° F.) and put in a warm place overnight. In summer, just 8 hours will do. Winter requires about 14 hours.

This soaking water is chock full of certain ingredients that will wash out your arteries as nothing else! Drink the juice. Afterwards, wash the seeds, roll up in a Turkish towel and keep damp. You must keep the seeds damp. Gradually, in the Turkish towel, note that the seeds sprout and grow. When they grow nice and long, remove from the towel (which is always to be kept damp) and eat — seed, root and stem. This will sweep out the toxic wastes from your insides.

Both alfalfa seed water and alfalfa seed sprouts in combo act like an internal housecleaning to wash away toxic residues that cling to your arteries. (Wait until green leaves are well developed before eating.) You can add to salads, sandwiches, soups.

My friendly neighbor farm woman underwent no other treatment to reduce her cholesterol level other than alfalfa seed sprouts and water. She lived to be a ripe 88 when I last saw her. I hope that she is still spry and youthful — she managed a small farm and a busy N.Y.C. hat shop, single-handed — if she is reading this book — and I hope she is still washing and oiling her arteries with the alfalfa sprout remedy.

TRY A STEAM BATH

How to flush out wastes through the millions of skin pores? Try a

Sauna bath. This dry heat method is popular in Finland. A Sauna room has a heater and a dehumidifier that can run up a temperature of 190°F, with only 3 percent humidity. You sit in such a room, your blood vessels dilate, and waste substances become moist and are passed off through the pores. A Sauna bath opens and dilates skin blood vessels, rushes blood through to the surface, getting rid of wastes through perspiration.

After a 10-minute session in a Sauna room, go over to a cool shower. The changes will cause constriction of the blood vessels, quick flushing of fat, cholesterol and waste through liver and kidneys for rapid elimination. This helps steam out your cholesterol deposits and put zing in your arteries.

If you can afford to have a Sauna room built in your house, so much the better. Otherwise, ask at your local health or athletic clubs if they have such facilities. Most large cities have them.

CLEANSE YOUR BRAIN

Senility is often traced to internal toxemia. Accumulated wastes cling to arteries that reach to your brain. Here's how it works. Within your brain is what is known as the "inner chamber" or *thalamus*. This is your subconscious. It is attached to some 13 billion cells and endless arteries that lead to the conscious centers of your brain cortex. Also, it joins to the deeper network of arteries and veins that make up the reticular formation of the brain stem, the coordinating system that sends impulses to your body to cause motion.

Here, this inner chamber, sends forth reflexes, emotions, thoughts, ideas, actions. When arteries become infested with waste substances, they cannot feed nourishment to the thalamus and signs of senility may ensue. Symptoms include nervous disorder, loss of memory, conflicts, premature aging.

Keep your brain in good working order by flushing out wastes that coat the inner arterial walls, narrowing them, making them hard and inelastic, incapable of carrying sufficient nutrition to the thalamus. Follow cholesterol-reducing tips in this chapter as part of your controlled fasting.

Highlights of Your Artery Oiling and Washing Program in Controlled Fasting

1. Arteries, capillaries, veins must be kept free of toxic wastes to better nourish your entire body, head to toe.
2. Dirty arteries reduce health, may lead to athersclerosis, arteriosclerosis or hardening of the arteries. Predisposes to heart attack, high blood pressure.
3. Cholesterol is a prime example of toxic waste.
4. Tobacco introduces more debris into the bloodstream.
5. Reduce animal fat intake, step up vegetable oils to wash out your arterial system.
6. Alfalfa sprouts in plant form and in water can both brush and wash out your insides.
7. Try a steam bath to flush out impurities through skin pores.
8. Better brain power is possible with cleaner arteries.

11

How to Turn Back
the Aging Clock
with Controlled Fasting

"I'd give anything to grow younger," sighed a woman in her early 50's, working at a job that might soon be taken over by a computer. "But my reflexes are slow, words get jumbled up, I just can't think straight."

She was only one of many women and men that I have met, and still meet, who wish they could turn back the hands of time. Well, that's kind of difficult. Science still has not broken the time barrier in our space age program. But I have found out that while you cannot turn back time by moving back the hands of a clock, or staring at a calendar of 10 years ago — you can embark upon a remarkably simple and remarkably effective controlled fasting plan that is aimed at revitalizing your body and mind, and thereby forestalling premature aging.

The woman mentioned above did surrender her job to a computer — but she was given a promotion to another job that will hardly be snapped by any machine because of its personalized nature. How did it happen?

I told her about a little-known way of washing out the toxic substances that cause a drop in blood sugar. The condition is known as hypoglycemia or "below normal blood sugar." *Hypo* means below or lower than normal — *glycemia* means sugar in the bloodstream.

This condition of internal toxemia can create mental and physical havoc and age you before your calendar years.

HYPOGLYCEMIA ... WHAT IT IS

It's normal for your blood sugar to fluctuate. In your blood is a substance known as glucose — a "toxic waste" substance that must be utilized and then discarded. Normal blood sugar level is 80 milligrams to 100 milligrams per 100 cubic centimeters of blood. Higher than this amount means that you have too much waste in your blood that cannot be disposed of. Lower than this amount means that waste products elsewhere in your body are preventing a normal amount of glucose into your bloodstream. This see-saw level and low blood sugar is called hypoglycemia. (The opposite of hypoglycemia is diabetes.)

SYMPTOMS

These are varied, sometimes bizarre. They range from feelings of fatigue, nervousness, irritability, depression, apprehension, excessive weakness, light-headedness, fainting spells, chronic insomnia, confusion, various states of emotional and mental disturbances. Many hypoglycemia victims who have this condition show signs of premature aging. Many are ousted from their jobs because they act and look old. That is what internal toxemia can do.

CONTROLLED FASTING PLAN TO NORMALIZE BLOOD SUGAR

Certain foods help normalize blood sugar, others create internal toxic states that are harmful. Here is a little plan, based upon findings by John W. Tintera, M.D. *(N.Y. State Journal of Medicine,* Vol. 55, No. 13):

FOODS ALLOWED

All meats, fish and shellfish. Dairy products. Recommended is 1 pint to one quart of acidophilus milk daily. You may need a doctor's prescription in some states for this type of milk. Inquire at your local dairy store. Allowed are all vegetables, all fruits, except those listed below. Eat peanut butter, Sanka, weak tea, sugar-free sodas, soybeans and soybean products, artificial sweeteners.

FOODS TO AVOID

Potatoes, corn, macaroni, spaghetti, rice, pie, cake, pastries, sugar, candies, dates and raisins, cola and other artificially sweetened soft drinks, coffee and strong tea, all hot and cold cereals (except occasionally oatmeal), alcoholic beverages, narcotics and drugs which act as stimulant or depressant.

What about bread? Devitalized white flour breads send carbohydrates and its ensuing waste formations into the bloodstream. Seek out starch-free American-Jerusalem artichoke flour bread. It has some oat flour, gluten and soya flour. Ask at a health store. Keep young and waste-free with this type of bread.

YOUR YOUTH TONIC

Here is a great internal flush-out drink, rich in precious minerals, vitamins and enzymes. Combine together one half apricot juice and one half apple juice. Add two tablespoons of apple cider vinegar. Add one tablespoon of coconut juice. Mix thoroughly or in a blender. Drink this before breakfast, before lunch, before dinner. (That is, one hour before each meal to let the ingredients wash out your insides before you introduce more food.) You'll find, as did myself, it really perks up your body and your mind.

PUT UP YOUR FEET

I initiated this program in a sales office where the executives complained of leg cramps and premature tiredness. It's an old-fashioned remedy but it has a strange way of working to stimulate the bloodstream and lubricate the arteries and free waste substances from accumulation.

Blood circulation, while primarily accomplished by the heart, is aided by tiny muscles within the artery walls and large arm and leg muscles. These arteries carry blood from heart to the body. If toxic-laden, they constrict or narrow.

These veins have no tiny muscles of their own. They depend upon your arm and leg muscles to send fresh blood back to your heart. If you stand or sit most of the day, blood tends to pool in the long veins of your legs. Toxic wastes and poisonous substances will cause some feeling of ache, sometimes swelling because of the downward pressure of the column of waste-laden blood that is stalled in the veins to the ankles and feet.

VARICOSE VEINS

These unsightly things are accumulations of toxic wastes — some fluid bearing these wastes escaped from your veins and capillaries into the ankle and leg tissues. Often, toxicity (body poisons) is felt in the calf muscles and ankles.

Lift Up Your Feet. Put them on your desk, or on a footstool. This drains the veins of the toxic blood that has been ballooning them, easing the ache of swollen legs and ankles. Lift them higher than your heart to favor return blood flow to the heart, aided by gravity. Foot elevation aids in the filling of the heart, circulation improvement, draws away debris-laden blood from its stagnant pool in the arteries and veins of your ankle.

A rocking chair and footstool used in combo is good. The chair helps the leg muscles free the stagnant blood from its ankles, to the stream of life. The footstool helps by gravity.

This simple trick drains stagnant blood from the legs, oxygenates it in the lungs, refreshes and purifies the blood before it returns to circulation.

Slant boards are sold in many department stores and health stores; you can lie with your head lower than your body. Keep your feet up and relax your brain, too. It shifts debris-laden blood from your feet, sends it back into the bloodstream to be washed clean and refreshed, and then sent to your brain to give you a feeling of alertness and youth.

**Rejuvenate Yourself with These Suggestions
During Controlled Fasting**

1. Premature aging is traced to hypoglycemia, a condition of low blood sugar and waste formations in the bloodstream.
2. Follow the do's and don'ts, designed to normalize blood sugar level.
3. Wash out debris in your blood channels with the special Youth Tonic.
4. Lift your feet up, on a desk, footstool, over your head. Free the stagnant toxic-laden wastes of blood and wash out your insides.

12

How to Cope with Arthritis with Controlled Fasting

Those concerned about the problem of health cannot avoid a feeling of deep compassion for the many millions who suffer through life with arthritis. These unfortunates have undergone one treatment after another with varying results. They are at a loss to know what next to do. Many hopes and expectations are raised when mention is made of a new discovery or technique that will enable them to live with arthritis. Who dares to hope about a method that will enable them to cope successfully with arthritis? This method is not a dream, not an illusion, but a reality. This method is based upon the ancient principles of controlled fasting that is designed to cleanse the cartilage and tissues that have become debris-ridden with toxic wastes and refuse, that impede free movement of limbs and create an arthritic condition. This is a doctor-tried method which I'll present you very shortly, in complete detail. It works! It can give you that blessed state of happiness — *relief from arthritis and its effects.*

ARTHRITIS NOT A MODERN DISEASE

Arthritis is an ancient problem. This form of degenerative joint disease can be seen in fossils of reptiles that died some 100 million years ago; it is seen in the remains of Stone Age man. In fact, the Pharaohs of ancient Egypt, too, fell victim to this problem.

The Greeks supplied one name, arthritis (from *arthron,* joint, and *itis,* inflammation), but not all victims have so-called arthritic inflammation.

Medieval doctors adopted another Greek term, *rheumatikos* (from *rheuma,* flow) because they believed the problem stemmed from a flow of noxious "humors" (fluids) into the joints.

Today, we know that arthritis and rheumatism are not single, definable ailments but terms that are vaguely applied to disorders in and around the joints. In fact, they comprise some 83 related ills listed by a committee of the American Rheumatism Association.

Arthritic disorders are costly, too; they lead to serious disabilities. In fact, they are second only to mental illness as a cause of lasting handicaps. They take a heavier toll of work days lost in industry than do accidents! Yearly, more than $15 million is spent in research for a cure. Over $300 million yearly is spent for medication. The search continues to find relief for arthritis. Let's take a closer look at this baneful ailment so we shall presently understand how a unique doctor-proven plan was able to provide a *drug-free relief* with controlled fasting.

Rheumatoid Arthritis. Close to 5 million victims, it attacks three times as many women as men, with a peak incidence at a young 35. Still's disease, another form, as well as ankylosing spondylitis (spinal arthritis) strikes young men under 35. This form of arthritis, that is, rheumatoid arthritis, involves acute and painful inflammation of several or all major joints. It leads to inflammation and thickening of the lining of the joints. The lining may grow into the space and fill it. Meanwhile the cartilage covering the ends of the bones may become eroded; often the bones may become brittle and pitted.

Early symptoms are fatigue, muscular stiffness, poor appetite, weight loss. Painful swelling then begins at one or more joints; nodules, from the size of a pea to a walnut, may appear under the skin. Muscular wasting and spasm often occur. Sometimes, fever takes place.

Osteoarthritis. While not inflammatory, it is a degenerative joint disease that feels warm to the touch. Sometimes, it is not felt at the start and is dangerously deceptive as it grows. According to Cecil and Loeb's *Textbook of Medicine,* it is a "baffling and fascinating" paradox. "A patient with advanced degenerative joint disease may have few or no complaints, whereas another patient showing only minor changes may be most uncomfortable." This arthritic form is characterized mainly by degeneration of joint cartilage. This becomes soft and wears unevenly. In some areas it may wear away completely, exposing the underlying bone and thickening of the ends of the bones may occur.

Early symptoms are stiffness, pain and aches, especially when the affected joint is vigorously used. Wear and tear increase pain severity; that is why farmers, manual laborers and assembly-line workers fall victim to this ailment more than one who sits most of the time. Vigorous movement affects the cartilage and membranes lining and surrounding the joints. Losing their original glassy smoothness, they become rough and fibrous; clefts and pits appear, followed by erosion, until the cartilage is worn away. Bone rubs against bone. This causes creaking and crackling in the joints — and pain.

Non-articular rheumatism. This takes in a host of problems which do not lie in the joints but in the attacked tendons and muscles. As an example, we know of *bursitis* — the bursae are closed sacs that contain something like brake fluid which serve as roller cushions for overlying tendons or muscles. Nature put these bursae in many body parts and they must get cleaned in order to work properly. They may fill up with a chalky goo or become very painful when the goo becomes hard and forms sharp waste deposits like stalactites in caves.

When these internal wastes are left in the body, related conditions are inflammation of a tendon sheath (tenosynovitis), inflammation of the tendon itself or surrounding tissue (tendinitis and peritendinitis), inflammation of bony projections at the elbow and knee (epicondylitis) and muscle inflammation (myositis). There is also fibrositis or muscular rheumatism and lumbago which is fibrositis in the low back and lumbar region of the body.

WHO SAYS IT ISN'T ARTHRITIS?

Do not be deluded into thinking you may not have arthritis. Here are some disorders which may develop from a waste-laden body and may be early advance warnings of arthritis:

Housemaid's or rug cutter's knee: inflammation of the bursa in front of the kneecap. Mailman's or nurse's foot: gradual falling of the foot's arch with pain from unnatural changes in the joints' bearing surfaces. Soldier's or policeman's heel: bursitis at the Achilles' tendon in the back of the foot. Glass or pitcher's or golfer's arm: inflammation in the bursa under the subdeltoid muscle covering the shoulder. Sportsman's shoulder: tendinitis or bursitis from repeated recoil of rifle or shotgun. Golfer's wrist and ballet dancer's ankle: tendinitis. Tennis elbow: caused with almost equal frequency by tendinitis, bursitis and epicondylitis and often by a combo. Driver's shoulder: osteoarthrosis from shifting stiff gears — eliminated for many drivers by automatic transmissions but not for over-the-road truckers or operators of heavy equipment. Driver's thigh: sciatic neuralgia from pressure on the thigh during continued immobility of the gas-pedal foot. Riveter's wrist (or jackhammer joints); osteoarthritis from the constant pounding of those infernal racketing machines. Weaver's bottom: bursitis of the ischial tuberosities (meaning the rear-most bones in your rump).

For all these conditions there is a variety of treatment, mostly of doubtful value, and as if arthritis and rheumatism were not confusing enough, the same patient will respond at different times in opposite ways to the same treatment for the same condition in the same joint!

So, if you are living in a false sense of security that arthritis may strike the next fellow, be not deceived. Re-read the preceding paragraphs and see how many different types of arthritis there are and picture yourself as a potential victim.

"Oh, it won't happen to me," is the typical attitude. "I take good care of myself." Good for you. We might add that former President Dwight D. Eisenhower also took good care of himself and underwent specialized treatment at government hospitals. Yet, at the age of 75, long after he retired from public office, he started to complain of pains in his joint. He was treated at Washington's Walter Reed Army Medical Center. The public diagnosis? He had painful and swollen wrists and hands, a touch of arthritis in the left knee (presumably the result of an old football injury), bursitis in the left elbow and some difficulty in his right shoulder. And here was a man who received the top medical care under the best supervision.

At the same time, a housewife will gasp, groan and grimace with pain when she gets on her knees in a simple housecleaning chore. She, too, is an arthritic victim. It can and does happen to almost anyone!

INTERNAL TOXEMIA THE VILLAIN IN ARTHRITIS?

A condition of a poison-laden bloodstream and toxic waste accumulation may be responsible for arthritis. We can understand this by understanding more about the ways the bones, cartilage and bloodstream work together to keep joints young and supple.

The adjoining ends of the bones are covered with *cartilage* — a semi-soft elastic tissue that cushions the joints and reduces friction and strain. The inner surface of the joint cavity is lined with a membrane known as the *synovial membrane* which issues a light, yellowish, semi-liquid fluid that keeps the joints lubricated. The ligaments and muscles hold the joint together and in place. This fluid MUST be clean, *free of toxic waste and debris*.

Healthy bones are firm and well-knit. There is no restriction to the circulation of the blood and lymph (a clear, straw-colored fluid that carries away toxic wastes from the tissues through a network known as the lymphatic system) which carries food and oxygen to the tissues while picking up internal toxic substances for elimination.

Healthy and waste-free cartilages are pliable and protect joints against excess strain of friction. Healthy and waste-free synovial membranes will issue a healthy and clean fluid that will lubricate the joints. Under such a free-from-toxemia condition, the ligaments and muscles have tonicity and springiness for firmness and balance.

When toxic wastes accumulate, the joints become large or swollen; they may shrivel up and waste. The bones become thick. The adjoining surfaces look irregular, rough, jagged. Blood and lymph circulation is filled with stagnant wastes; tissues are therefore deprived of oxygen and nutrition. This disrupts the entire valuable and delicately precious process of eliminating waste materials.

Cartilages lose their pliability, become dry and brittle. The function of the synovial membrane is also impeded, clogged. There is a faulty secretion process. If internal toxemia is left unchecked, the membrane may be worn out; secretion dries up completely. The muscles and ligaments lose flexibility and tone, wasting away or becoming congested with refuse and thick with slough. These conditions do not occur overnight, neither do they all strike at once. It is a gradual health loss. Slowly, as the disease progresses, the destructive changes become more advanced. Internal toxemia takes its toll in this insidious manner.

CONTROLLED FASTING IS ESSENTIAL TO BATTLE ARTHRITIS

While medication is beneficial, ranging from aspirin to surgery—there is no cure! Everyone tells you that you can live with arthritis but until now (you'll be given this drugless method in a few pages) no one tells you how you can begin to live *without* arthritis burdening you. The first step is that of controlled fasting which helps rid your body of poisonous by-products. As you have learned in this volume, the body organs become clogged up. They need to adequately eliminate the waste products and toxins that have accumulated. Controlled fasting helps to wash out the cartilages, purify the lymphatic system, clean the synovial membranes that must be sparkling fresh if arthritis is to be banished in one form or another. Toxins need to be disposed of so over-all body metabolism is fully restored.

THE "W-W" FAST PLAN

A bold and successful internal cleansing plan has been developed by a team of physicians who sought to end and cure arthritis rather than have victims rely upon drugs that alleviate pain but do not banish the condition. This plan, which I term the "W-W" Fast Plan (Waste-Washing), is so exciting, I fervently hope it will become the long, sought-after, drugless way for combatting arthritis for possible cure, sparing millions of painful lives.

The system was reported to the *Journal of the National Medical Association,* by Charles A. Brusch, M.D. and Edward T. Johnson,

M.D., who tried this "W-W" fast plan as I term it, and the success rate is remarkable.

The method of controlled fasting produced major clinical and hematological (blood) improving conditions in arthritis and rheumatism. The main points of this Plan are the taking of cod liver oil on an empty stomach and the restriction of all water intake to a single portion taken one hour before breakfast.

Originally, the doctors selected 140 patients; a few dropped out for various reasons, so the tests were given to 98 who could follow the complete plan. The doctors reported that 92 patients showed major improvement in their arthritic symptoms and wonderful changes in their blood cleanliness. The blood sedimentation (toxic wastes and debris) dropped down. Cholesterol levels were normalized, even though this controlled fasting plan allowed eggs, butter, milk and cod liver oil. Blood sugar levels "turned to the lower side of normal." One diabetic patient gave up taking insulin. Blood pressure was also normalized.

The doctors state clearly that "there was a complete curtailment of soft drinks, candy, cake, ice cream or any food made up of white sugar ... Those who felt that the sacrifice of coffee was too great were allowed black coffee — 15 minutes before breakfast."

BASIC PLAN

For a period of six months, the arthritics did not eat any foods that contained white sugar; for most of them, no coffee. Here are the other diet rules:

1. All daily water intake was consumed solely upon arising, preferably at warm or room temperatures and one hour before breakfast.
2. With meals, the only liquids allowed were room temperature milk or warm soup (not creamed). Throughout the day, these were the only liquids permitted to quench thirst.
3. Cod liver oil, mixed either with two tablespoonfuls of fresh, strained orange juice or two tablespoonfuls of cool milk was taken at these times:
   (a) One hour before breakfast.
   (b) Thirty minutes after water intake.

(c) Five hours after the evening meal.

(d) A short time before retiring for the night.

Diabetics and those with heart ailments took the oil only twice weekly. All others took the mixture every single day. The cod liver oil mixtures were shaken well in a screw-top glass before taking.

4. Any food supplements or tablets or pills could be taken either with the water upon arising, with milk or soup at mealtime, or with milk or soup at any time. Remember — milk or soup were the only allowable beverages to the arthritic patients except for the morning water.

5. No sugar or any sugar-containing food was allowed at any time.

6. No coffee except before breakfast.

INTERNAL CLEANSING

The sugar-free diet may have done the trick in this "W-W" Fast Plan. Sugar is a highly concentrated carbohydrate from which all the water has been removed. That is why it cakes so quickly in a damp climate and absorbs water. The arthritic (or anyone else) who eats sugar-containing foods will want water and this causes the internal absorption as sugar drains water from the tissues, depriving them of nourishment. Sugar leaves a waste residue, a toxic ash which contaminates the insides and this may lead to arthritic symptoms.

This special plan actually washed out the insides of the patients and helped bring about relief and possible cure!

The doctors refer to another controlled fasting plan created by a Doctor Pemberton back in the 1920's. He treated 400 arthritic patients on the cod liver oil therapy "provided the patients were kept away from 'inferior type' starches." These are the foods made with sugar and bleached flours, and never have a place in controlled fasting.

OTHER BENEFITS RECORDED

After internal cleansing was performed, in addition to arthritic relief and cure, other benefits were recorded: noticeable skin improvement, better hair and scalp health, cerumen (ear wax) correction, diminishing of inflammatory ear conditions, favorable blood cleansing, and urine changes.

The doctors later stated, "We felt these (rapid) improvements were due primarily to the cod liver oil and unusual arrangements for liquid drinking intake. While it is true that these favorable objective and laboratory findings would eventually appear with a favorable diet (alone), the relativity of time to obtain these more or less same results would differ. We obtain our results in three to six months time. A wholesome diet alone would perhaps take six to thirty-six months to produce 50 to 75% of our results at best."

So it appears that the cod liver oil and water restriction helped to wash out the insides. A sugar-free diet kept the insides from further accumulations of waste substances. This sugar-free diet alone would help retain internal cleanliness but the cod liver oil and water plan speeded up the process.

DIFFERENCES IN TYPES OF WATER

You may say that water is water and it does help wash out the insides with no particular difference. The doctors reported that there is a difference in waters, though. While the digestive tract cannot tell the difference, "their surface tensions are considerably different; tap water having the highest surface tension level and fruit and vegetable water content being of the low range of surface tension levels."

In other words, freshly drawn tap water taken as the doctors suggest, can really clean off the accumulated slough and internal grime with more effectiveness than fruit and vegetable water content.

Also, water taken from an apple or a carrot requires from one to four hours to wash through the digestive tract. The doctors point out that water "taken on an empty stomach as suggested, would be delivered in the system in a matter of minutes — not hours."

The doctors found that internal sedimentation and toxic wastes were speedily flushed out of the system and through the kidneys if water were taken upon arising and liquid drinking controlled as per their methods.

The doctors also suggest a wholesome diet that is *free from refined foods*. All foods should be of a natural, unprocessed source!

So there we have an arthritic diet — a Waste-Washing Fast Plan that successfully combatted arthritis!

BROWN BREAD TECHNIQUE

Because bones are constructed of minerals, they need a steady supply of these precious nutrients. You should take advantage of brown bread — unbleached, unprocessed, natural. A storehouse of minerals for your bones. Any arthritic who wants to eat bread should eliminate all breads made from white or bleached or processed flours and devote himself to brown bread. You will surely enjoy this rich, natural and juicy taste and your skeletal structure will benefit by the intake of minerals, available at most health stores and special diet shops.

The many millions upon millions of arthritic victims will welcome relief and possible cure. Controlled fasting may be that solution.

Joint-Ease Guide Lines

1. There are more than 80 different forms of arthritis ranging from stiff fingers to complete invalidism in a hospital. At the first warnings signs, look to internal cleansing.
2. A poison-drenched bloodstream, toxic-laden cartilage condition, dirty synovial membranes predispose to arthritic complications.
3. The "W-W" Fast Plan — Waste Washing System — is designed to rid your body of toxic waste accumulations. Try the internal cleansing technique as utilized by two physicians.
4. Step up mineral intake with brown bread. Eliminate all refined foods. Eliminate refined sugar in all forms.

13

How to Combat Allergies
with Controlled Fasting

When I was in my teens, I found myself "catching cold" every August. This "cold" would last until October or the first frost. Each year, until I was around 20, I caught the same "cold" and noticed that it grew in severity. I would sneeze, cough, sputter, toss and turn nightly during the hot summer months because of a clogged and stuffy nose. My eyes would run, my hearing was faulty. It was downright uncomfortable not to mention distressing. That was when I decided to see a doctor who listened to my tale of woe and said simply, "You've got an allergy — hay fever."

What to do? He filled me with pills, concoctions, inhalation remedies, injections, etc. My symptoms were eased and I stopped my sneezing — but I became a drug addict. No, not in the narcotic sense that you're thinking. Instead, I was enslaved to the pills and medicines and the weekly injection that left me feeling dizzy, nervous and irritable. I had no choice, I was told, because hay fever does not usually just go away — worse than that, if untreated, it develops into asthma. Once this happens, other allergies start to follow. In a desperate effort to free myself from my allergy, I delved into endless books, met with physicians, specialists in diet and controlled fasting and came up with a special method that reduced my symptoms to a point where I could actually stop all my medication and enjoy breathing without an unnatural sneeze. It took me years to develop serious hay fever that almost erupted into asthma, so a possible cure is still in the works as I write this chapter. But a cure is on its way and by the time you read this chapter, I hope I'll have succeeded in chasing away your allergies with a special controlled fasting plan that I'll divulge presently.

WHAT IS ALLERGY?

The word is derived from the Greek *allos,* meaning "other" plus *ergon,* meaning "work," a loose interpretation is that "another work" is causing an adverse internal reaction.

It is not a new ailment. The very first recorded allergy case is believed to have occurred in 2641 B.C. Hieroglyphics on Egyptian tablets of time record the death of King Menes from a hornet's sting. Apparently, His Highness was allergic to a substance "injected" by the insect. Of course, allergic ailments are not always fatal but they can trigger off a serious condition.

Allergic diseases rank third in prevalence among chronic ailments. More than 24 million persons have allergies which include asthma, hay fever, migraine headaches, eczema and sensitivity to dye, drug, insect, inhalant, etc.

According to Herman Hirschfeld, M.D., founder and director of New York's Allergy Testing Laboratory, "Any conceivable substance is capable of causing an allergic reaction in someone. Some people eat their allergens (allergic substances), some sniff them, some inherit them, some touch them and others are injected with them. We know that allergy causes cataracts of the eye in some people, fatigue in others, and research may prove that schizophrenia and depression can be allergic in origin!"

HOW ALLERGIES STRIKE

Allergies usually show up on your bronchial tree which is related to your nose. Within your chest cavity are your bronchial tubes which connect the windpipe (trachea); they send air to your lungs. This air comes in through your nose.

Your bronchial tubes look like tree roots. The large bronchial tubes divide into smaller and smaller ones until they become tubes that are finer than threads. Each one ends in a tiny air space. Here, the air you breathe comes into close contact with the thin-walled capillaries which carry blood through the lungs.

The tiny air spaces and lung capillaries make up a very important area. It is here that oxygen from the air enters the blood. In this same area, waste gas (carbon dioxide) is removed from the lungs and breathed out. You breathe in and out about 16 times each minute.

When you breathe in an irritating or offensive substance, your bronchial tubes react with resistance, triggering off an allergic attack. This distress is caused by the narrowing of these bronchial tubes. Three changes take place to reduce the size of the smaller bronchial tubes. One is the contraction of the muscle fibers in the walls of the tubes. The second is the swelling of the cells in the membranes that line the air tubes. The third change is an excessive amount of mucus accumulating in the tubes from over-active bronchial glands.

During an attack, breathing is like trying to force air through a tube with a clamp on it. The bronchial muscles have a spasm and the unfortunate victim has a feeling that he is choking to death! Of course, he will not die but the fear is enough to make him sensitive, weak; if he has a heart condition, it can be very serious, indeed.

TYPICAL ALLERGIES

These include asthma which affects more than 5 million. Repeated asthmatic attacks and forced breathing stretches the lung tissues and may cause permanent damage. If this happens, the asthmatic has less endurance and may experience short breath on the slightest exertion. An extra load is placed on the heart which must now work harder to force blood through the damaged lungs.

Hay fever affects 1 out of every 20, or over 8 million persons. It makes life miserable. It is caused by a sensitivity to the ragweed pollen — given off by the ragweed plant. In asthma, an attack is caused by various dusts, cosmetics, powders, sudden inhalation of cold air, irritating substances. In hay fever, usually the ragweed pollen is the sole offender. Symptoms are alike, generally.

Hives (urticaria) is an allergic skin reaction in which pale, raised welts appear together with intense itching. This may be traced to certain foods, outside influences, clothing and a score of offenders.

CELLULAR WASTES

The main fact about allergies is that the mucous-membrane structures and the skin are super-saturated with uneliminated cellular excretions. The body must be cleansed of these impurities by means of controlled fasting.

This method is very potent in cleaning out cellular skin wastes and the mucous membranes. Poisonous wastes and toxic substances as well as internal debris that cause irritation and inflammation need to be flushed out in a special plan. Your bloodstream must also be washed. After all, the bronchial tubes are exposed to your bloodstream together with your other body organs.

When a cellular waste or foreign substance is not passed off, it remains in your bloodstream and leads to an allergic condition. The basis for relief of allergy lies in controlled fasting. Your body attempts to neutralize or wash out these poisonous wastes by sending forth histamine. It is this histamine that triggers off an allergic reaction. Your body cannot accommodate histamine in over-abundant quantities and you suffer the symptoms.

Dr. Elbert Tokay, author of *The Human Body,* observes, "There is some evidence that many allergic reactions of the body result from the liberation of histamine or a like substance in the body. Histamine is known to dilate small blood vessels and make them more permeable. These events could be responsible for such phenomena as skin eruptions and runny noses. Any substance which would inactivate histamine would prevent these symptoms." Controlled fasting may well be that "substance."

THE INTERNAL CLEANSING TEA

Let's meet *fenugreek* — an herb used by the ancient people of the Mediterranean and Asiatic worlds. According to the dictionary, fenugreek is an "Old World aromatic herb of the bean family, having sickle-shaped pods containing edible, mucilaginous seeds." Here is a herb tea that has the ability to cleanse out your insides. In fact, when I first learned of this tea, I found that nothing else could do the trick with such effectiveness.

The fenugreek seeds are said to be equal in value to quinine for fever reduction; it soothes inflamed stomachs and intestines, it cleanses the stomach, bowels, kidneys as well as the respiratory tract. A tea infused from the fenugreek seed is delicious as well as fragrant. When fenugreek seeds are moistened, they become slightly sticky (mucilaginous). The tea has the ability to soften and dissolve other sticky substances and cleanse the bloodstream.

How fenugreek works. Compare your body to an auto engine that has become caked with sludge. Your mechanic uses a "flushing oil" to cleanse out the hardened accumulations of grease and dirt from the engine. In other words, one oil has to dissolve another oil or grease. Or, one mucilaginous substance must dissolve another. That is how the slightly sticky viscosity of fenugreek tea is able to soften and dissolve hardened masses of accumulated wastes and toxins that cause internal sensitivity.

The secret is that the action cleanses and soothes the insides by softening, dissolving and re-coating with a healing substance.

Waste-laden bloodstream. Toxic wastes saturate the bloodstream, make it thick and sluggish. The blood suffers from poor circulation; oxygen cannot be transported to the cells. The blood is unable to carry away waste matter from the cells speedily enough to prevent their becoming contaminated. Excess wastes and mucus must be disposed of — either through sneezing, coughing, copious tears, pimples, boils, allergic symptoms or else the wastes go to the stomach, intestines and kidneys. Here, the toxic substances accumulate, harden and now a general health breakdown is in evidence.

Internal reaction. The stomach lining has thousands of small openings. Waste substances lodge into these openings, causing an irritation. More internal mucus is secreted by the stomach lining in an effort to relieve the irritation and this sets off an allergic symptom. (The same happens when a dirt particle gets into the eye and the tear ducts send out moisture to wash it out.)

An accumulation of waste leads to fermentation and faulty digestion.

Fenugreek tea has the ability to gradually soften, then dissolve this unwanted coating of internal toxemia, washing out the digestive system, washing out the bloodstream.

POWER OF FENUGREEK

The herbal plant that produces the fenugreek seeds is rich in volatile oils which are transported to the seeds. When these oils appear in a brew, they can seek out and penetrate the most remote nooks and crevices of the membranous body linings; the oils are also absorbed into the cellular tissues and work to wash out the delicate capillaries and leave them sparkling clean. Some of the oils also find their way into the sweat glands, cleanse and revitalize them so pores of the skin are likewise washed and cleansed.

CONTROLLED FASTING PLAN

Fenugreek seeds (sold at health stores and also in tea bag at some stores) make a delicious and wholesome beverage. Before an allergic attack, drink a cup or two of the tea. After an attack, drink two cups. For a period of 30 days, drink no other hot beverage other than fenugreek tea! This helps wash out your insides.

How to make: put two tablespoonfuls of fenugreek seeds into one cup of bubbly-boiled water. Let steep for six minutes. Stir well. Strain or let the seeds settle at the bottom. You may sweeten with a dab of honey or lime juice. Sip slowly.

You will soon feel the wonderful effects. Fenugreek tea removes and rinses off the accumulation of stagnant mucous secretions throughout your body.

To revitalize your body and enjoy internal cleansing, here are six steps to follow.

SIX STEP HEALTH BUILDING PLAN

1. A sudden change from hot to cold (both internal and external) will react upon the sensitive blood vessels in the breathing apparatus, making them more delicate and vulnerable to an allergy attack. When going out in the cold air, cover your nasal passages by holding a handkerchief to your nose. This "filters" cold air so it will be pleasantly mild and warm as it is breathed in. Avoid sudden or extreme temperature changes.

2. When bathing, use lukewarm or hot water. NEVER use cold

water. Avoid cold swimming pools or ocean waters. Avoid chlorinated or chemically treated pools since foreign substances are introduced via breathing and pores and further clog up your insides. Further, the shock of cold water will lower your body metabolism and temperature, creating more sensitivity to allergens. Your daily washing should also be with warm water.

3. All foods (liquids and solids) should be warm or at room temperature. Ice cold drinks constrict the delicate arterial naso-pharynx and bronchial structures, making them sensitive. An allergic attack is often triggered when the system is shocked by cold drinks. Avoid soft drinks, carbonated beverages, ice cream, foods with refined white sugars and refined flours, sweets, chocolates, coffee. These all introduce toxic wastes to your system.

4. Stay away from foods and beverages which have triggered your symptoms in the past. Hot spicy foods, alcohol, smoke, all irritate the system. If you sneeze while shaving or putting on makeup, change your brand of toiletries. Be careful not to accidentally sniff up a snootful of powder. This introduces toxic substances that irritate an already over-burdened bloodstream.

5. The so-called "convenience" foods such as pepper, salt, catsup, mustard, vinegar and all foods containing these waste-forming foods should be eliminated from your diet. By their harsh reaction in your system, they enter the delicate and fragile blood vessels. Ever notice how "hot" you feel after eating foods that have been seasoned? Your temperature raises as your body metabolism works to dispose of the cellular wastes, then plummets down when you "cool off." This see-saw shift, by the way, plays havoc with your blood pressure and may erupt into an allergic symptom. Avoid all harsh condiments.

6. Just as your body should not be heated up by the clutter of residue left by spicy foods, neither should it become unnecessarily chilled. The indoor temperature should be no more than 12°F. below the outside air because extreme cooling may irritate the nasal and bronchial tube membranes. The hands and feet of the allergic persons should ALWAYS be kept comfortably warm! If these body parts feel cold, it means there is a heavy blood congestion and toxic accumulation in other body parts. This unnatural blood congestion of waste debris is often a precursor of an allergy attack. To draw blood away from other parts, to evenly distribute the blood and ease congestion of waste accumulations, soak both

hands and feet in a tub of hot water. Comfortably hot, that is. Gradually, the heat draws blood back to your cold limbs, freeing the congestion, making you less susceptible to allergic symptoms.

WHOLE CONCEPT INVOLVED
WITH CONTROLLED FASTING

A complete concept is involved in handling allergies successfully. A television actress lost out on many assignments because she was always breaking out into asthmatic attacks at crucial filming moments. She was on the verge of losing everything when she heard of my proposed book on fasting and allergic problems. She tried the fenugreek method and experienced enough relief to get some good television jobs. But she kept up her other debris-accumulation habits; that is, she ate commercialized white flour foods, sugar, artificially tampered foods. She finally gave up everything in disgust saying that the tea didn't help her all the way and she was going to quit the acting business. I think she did because I don't see her around the studios any more. I tried to explain to her that a "whole concept" is involved in the controlled fasting therapy plan. You must cleanse out your entire body and that involves a complete housecleaning.

You cannot clean your house by wiping one corner of the floor. You cannot clean your car by wiping the brake. You cannot clean out your body by just one little step. You must follow the entire plan and then you may expect to experience success. I know this is true because I follow every step in this particular chapter and my hay fever (which almost developed into bronchial asthma) has subsided almost to the curative point. It should work for you. Give it a chance!

Allergic Housecleaning Tips

1. Allergies, including asthma, hay fever, skin ailments, are often

traced to a dirt-laden bloodstream that is soaked with foreign substances that cause internal irritation.

2. Clean out your bloodstream, wash your irritant-soaked cells and tissues with fenugreek tea.

3. Follow each and every step in the 6-step plan of controlled fasting to cleanse your insides and strengthen resistance to allergies.

14

How Controlled Fasting Helps
Your Liver to Give You
Better Health

You have a built-in sieve through which all toxic wastes are filtered, neutralized and, in a sense, washed out of your body. This sieve is your liver. Here is an organ that is responsible for digestion and assimilation of food and charged with the powerful task of eliminating and/or detoxifying and neutralizing those remnants of internal toxemia. Clearly, a healthy liver can do much to assist you in your quest for a natural way to health through controlled fasting. A sick or clogged-up liver is like a debris-clogged sieve — function is impaired and waste products accumulate to undermine efficiency.

A LOOK AT YOUR FILTER ORGAN

That's right. Your liver is a filter, just as you have a filter in a motor or in a kitchen sink faucet. And you know what happens to the machinery when the filter gets clogged up. The same happens to the body machinery. Your fasting program has a wonderful opportunity for health-building success when your internal filter is cleansed and healthy.

Your liver is the largest organ in your body. In a young adult, it may weigh four times as much as your heart or two kidneys combined. It usually weighs about four pounds; it lies in the right upper part of the abdomen, just below the diaphragm and is covered for the most part by the lower ribs. Sometimes, you can feel its outer border under the ribs.

In a slight depression on the undersurface of the liver is found the gall bladder. Ducts from the liver join with the duct from the gall bladder to form a common bile duct that empties into the duodenum (part of the digestive canal).

What does your liver do? It's your built-in detoxification factory. Through the liver pass the oceans of toxin-laden wastes that must be cleansed, rendered neutral and given off. Each day, a healthy liver must manufacture and secrete bile, the substance that you need to digest food, especially fats. Your liver takes carbohydrates and stores these nutrients in the form of glycogen to be released into the bloodstream in the form of utilized sugar when needed for muscle and even thought energy.

Toxic wastes. An unhealthy or unclean sieve means that the liver cannot secrete enough bile so fats cannot be fully digested; a deposit of fat-film is formed on other ingested food which, in turn, become more difficult to digest. A further accumulation of waste debris seriously undermines overall body health.

Your liver must neutralize and render harmless the many irritating waste substances and toxins that accumulate in the body because of the metabolic processes and are introduced in the body via food, drink and air. When your internal sieve or filter becomes clogged up with debris, when it becomes sick, the overall body health begins to suffer.

Danger signs. In his book, *A Cancer Therapy,* the noted Max Gerson, M.D. refers to a statement made by another physician, Kasper Blond, who warned of these danger signs as related to a dirty sieve or human filter: "The whole syndrome of metabolic disorders which we call oesophagitis (inflammation of the esophagus), gastritis, duodenitis (inflammation of the duodenum), gastric and duodenal ulcer, cholecystitis (gallbladder inflammation), pancreatitis (inflammation of the pancreas), proctitis (inflammation of the rectum and prostate gland disorder), and others are considered only stages of a dynamic process, *starting with liver failure* and portal-hypertension (hardening of the blood vessels which provide the liver with its circulation), and resulting in cirrhosis (hardening) of the liver tissue, and sometimes in cancer."

When your liver becomes clogged up, it is comparable to sediment that you can see on a sieve or any filter — the filter apparatus becomes hard. This is similar to cirrhosis, traced to an unclean and toxin-laden liver. Other afflictions related to a clogged liver include diabetes, heart disease, kidney infection, circulatory and blood disorders.

SIX INTERNAL CLEANSING JOBS THE LIVER DOES

Before we find out how you can fortify yourself against liver ailment and how a special controlled fasting plan can wash out your insides, let's look at the six basic functions of this sieve:

1. *Food Digestion.* The liver produces bile which it pours into the intestines to help in fat digestion. The liver receives digested foods from the intestines and acts upon these. The liver changes certain sugars (levulose and galactose) into dextrose. The liver takes certain amino acids that cannot be used by the body and transforms them into waste products to be eliminated by the kidneys. Controlled fasting is based upon a sound and healthful eliminative process and that is where the liver comes into its precious purpose.

2. *Storehouse.* Digested sugars and starches are changed into glycogen and stored in liver cells to be changed into blood sugar by the liver when needed for body energy. A healthy and "washed" liver can do this properly. Otherwise, over-all energy begins to flutter. And that includes mental energy, too!

3. *Stores Iron.* This precious mineral is stored by the liver. Deficiencies of iron lead to anemia, tired blood, poor circulatory powers.

4. *Seizes Poisons.* In an effort to rid your body of certain toxic wastes, your liver will seize such poisons as lead and mercury; often, a weak liver succumbs to these poisons in the battle to get rid of them. A healthy internal filter is vital for toxic waste release.

5. *Neutralizes Toxic Wastes.* Your body either manufactures or receives certain poisons — as from tobacco smoke, gasoline fumes, substances in coffee, tea, alcohol, sharp condiments, etc. Your liver is charged with the responsibility of neutralizing these poisons, preparing them for elimination via the kidneys. You must have a clean liver that can "accept" certain wastes of intestinal origin,

detoxify these wastes coming from the colon and send them to the kidney for removal. As an example, we have a colon-originated gas known as *indol* — a by-product of incompletely assimilated eggs, meat and beans. This toxic waste is formed when it is in excess. In the liver, indol joins with certain substances to form *indican*, another waste that must be given off. It is found in certain ailments such as wasting diseases. The liver has the job of neutralizing the effects of this waste substance.

6. *Biliousness*. When the liver is saturated with excessive amounts of toxic wastes, this condition follows. It is symptomized by a feeling of tiredness, headache, poor appetite, weakness and even nausea.

CLEAN BILE

The process of internal detoxification depends upon clean bile — this is a liver-manufactured fluid that is stored and concentrated in the gall bladder. It acts as a fat solvent in the digestive process. A waste-laden bile-stream is brown to yellow in color. If it backs up into the bloodstream, it leads to jaundice.

Normally, bile is alkaline in reaction, contains certain enzymes which act as an antiseptic or bactericide. Bile neutralizes the acidity of substances poured into the intestine. Otherwise, the delicate inner membrane of the intestines become damaged because of this acidity of the gastric contents and this leads to erosion or ulceration.

If liver wastes and toxic substances saturate the bile, this means that the biliary tracts or channel leading to the gall bladder and into the intestine become obstructed and may lead to formation of gallstones. Once this happens, the liver is impaired by inflammation and degeneration.

Cleanses your bloodstream. As Dr. Logan Clendening in *The Human Body*, pointed out, "One of the chief functions of the liver is to detoxicate the blood before it gets elsewhere in the body. And the liver naturally suffers from its exposed position to the action of these various poisons. A healthy liver is a strong and active organ; and it can and does remove a large number of poisons from the blood, thus protecting us constantly from their affects, without damage to its own cells."

Of course, the habitual eating of rich, sweet and greasy foods, together with alcoholic liquors, clutters up the internal filter. One doctor said that people who suffer from liver disorders are able to cleanse themselves internally by abstaining from meat, living on a vegetarian diet. Elimination of all fatty and greasy foods is another step. All the blood from the intestines goes first through the liver — nearly 700 quarts daily — if there are toxins or irritants in the blood, the liver is affected.

Early symptoms include a loggy feeling, bowel sluggishness, headaches, a bitter taste (when bile is debris-laden, it may flow upward into the stomach), a furred (coated) tongue and poor appetite.

LIVER DISTRESS

According to Boyd's *Pathology of Internal Disease,* here is how toxins dirty up the liver cells: "The cells of the liver are bathed in the blood brought by the portal vein from the gastrointestinal tract, blood which may contain toxins known or unknown. The result of such toxic action may be the death of some or many of the cells of a liver lobule, it may be one or many of the lobules themselves."

Which toxic wastes have a cellular-destructive action? Dr. Boyd adds, "Among the numerous agents, most diverse in character, which may cause degeneration and necrosis of the liver cells may be mentioned chemicals, proteins and products of protein decomposition, bacterial toxins, foreign proteins and products of protein decomposition, bacterial toxins, infections and exposure to radiation."

Boyd points out that a *high fat intake* can overburden your internal filter with wastes, impairing liver function. There may follow interference in circulation, depriving cells of needed oxygen. When this happens, the liver cells are choked so efficient carbohydrate metabolism cannot take place, and the cells become clogged with fat which replaced the normal glycogen. If the liver cells do not get enough oxygen, there may be cirrhosis (hardening) or necrosis (death) of the liver cells.

UNPLEASANT AILMENTS

These include *cirrhosis* or liver hardening; *atrophy* or liver wasting; *hepatitis* or liver inflammation caused by accumulation of toxic wastes; *fatty degeneration* and *congestion* of the liver. In cirrhosis, the normal functioning cells become saturated with infective poisons and toxins, becoming replaced by hard and fibrous tissues. Alcoholic cirrhosis introduces many toxic wastes into the system and clogs up this delicate sieve.

Jaundice, also know as *icterus,* is traced to a debris-laden and waste-accumulated bile; symptoms are seen in which the whites of the eyes and even the mucous membranes turn yellow. This ailment is preceded when the body seeks to rid itself of accumulated poisons by means of gastro-intestinal upheaval, nausea and loss of appetite. *This last-named symptom is Nature's warning to consider controlled fasting.* Nature wants you to reduce your food intake, readjust yourself to healthful foods and give your body a chance to get rid of toxic wastes.

In fatty disease or liver degeneration, the cells of this internal filter become infiltrated with fat wastes. There is some enlargement of the organ too. Once again, we see that toxic wastes must be sloughed off, the liver must be strengthened and kept clean as a sieve should be clean if the filtering agent of your body is to serve you well.

FOODS TO OMIT

To clean your liver, your program for controlled fasting should rigidly exclude these foods: fat foods (butter, cream, eggs,) all fat meats and fat fish; spices, pepper, salt, mustard, catchup, vinegar and all condiments. Omit stimulants of every kind and this includes tea, coffee and chocolate. Omit alcohol. Omit all processed and refined foods. I might add that *herb teas* are satisfactory because they contain no tannic acid, a harsh internal irritant. Select caffeine-free coffee, too. Ask at a health store for these foods.

WASH YOUR FILTER

Two hours after each meal — which should be low in fat and low in starch — drink two glasses of one type of freshly squeezed fruit juice — or vegetable juice. The minerals and enzymes in the juices will exert an internal washing effect on your liver (filter) and you will help to keep it clean.

DESICCATED LIVER

Here is a remarkable and astonishingly powerful detoxifying food. Desiccated (dehydrated) liver is prepared in capsule and powder form by a special high-speed process. It is the whole liver with only certain connective tissue and fat removed, subjected to this high-speed process and then transformed into a capsule or a powder form. It is sold in almost all health stores.

Desiccated liver is superior to whole liver for some unexplainable reasons. Desiccated liver produces a certain enzyme in the intestines that acts as a detoxifying agent. It also seems to nullify certain poisonous substances that, in turn, protect against fatigue and help build blood health to resist anemia.

Writing in the *American Journal of Digestive Diseases*, Morton S. Biskind, M.D., tells how he was able to cleanse out the insides of subjects by means of this desiccated liver program. "When whole desiccated liver is used as a source of the as yet unidentified but essential nutritional factors, both trace minerals as well as a certain amount of protein of highest quality are simultaneously provided. Although, in actual practice, it has rarely been necessary to supplement such therapy by addition of further trace minerals, the mineral content of liver products must of course vary from batch to batch and it is not certain that the entire need for all trace minerals can always be supplied by this source. Hence, supplementation with these trace elements may often be advisable."

Desiccated liver is a storehouse of internal cleansing minerals and the effect can be strengthened with the addition of supplementation.

This brings us to *brewer's yeast* — Here is a substance that is made from yeast, subjected to a dehydrating process that does not disturb the precious store of B-complex vitamins and other toxic-fighting substances.

Dr. Biskind fed test subjects a combination of desiccated liver with brewer's yeast and was able to rejuvenate them — that's right — he was able to completely cleanse out their insides and make them all over again into lively and youthful vitality. Thus we can see the powerful effects of a healthy liver and a clean and washed out internal filter that is able to process and discard wastes and toxemia-residue.

YOUR ONE-DAY LIVER-CLEAN PLAN

Here is a simple step-by-step plan to follow in helping to wash out the toxic wastes that may be impairing the function of your internal filter, your liver:

1. Before breakfast, mix one tablespoon of brewer's yeast flakes with two tablespoons of desiccated liver extract in a 8 ounce glass of celery juice. Blend together carefully. Drink before breakfast.
2. Throughout the day, take *none* of these so-called foods: spices or condiments, sweets, stimulants (that includes coffee, tea, cocoa, alcohol), starches, fat foods (no butter, cream, eggs, fat meats).
3. Eat freely (but at separate meals) of raw or stewed fruits, raw or stewed vegetable. Brown rice or buckwheat groats and a small baked potato (without butter) is good for filling that empty feeling.
4. Try meatless foods — sold in convenient canned form at health stores.
5. For a nightcap, take the same combo described in Step 1.

You will discover that this internal cleansing plan, plus the remarkable internal-healing effects of desiccated liver and Brewer's yeast, helps to detoxify your insides and rejuvenate your entire body and mind.

HOW AN ACTIVE MANAGER
CONQUERED LIVER TROUBLE

Young Floyd, a department store floor manager, was troubled with a feeling of biliousness and developed a sallow skin. He felt weak, tired all the time, had to make more than normal trips to the rest lounge. He almost lost his job. He asked me about controlled fasting and decided to go on the above plan for a period of three days! It so rejuvenated him, he now follows this liver-clean plan, every single Tuesday. It's a wonderful way to detoxify his insides, particularly his liver.

You, too, may set aside one or two days weekly for this method of fasting to rejuvenate your liver. Incidentally, you can obtain desiccated liver and brewer's yeast at most any health store.

Try desiccated liver in capsule form — take six daily as part of your regular fare.

Because animal fats have an accumulative affect on the liver, you would do well to substitute with vegetable-source fats and oils.

CONTROLLED FASTING THERAPY FOR THE LIVER

You will discover a greater effect of this internal-cleansing plan if you *precede* and *follow* this "Liver-Clean" method by strict fasting. That is, the day before and the day after should be devoted exclusively to an intake of freshly squeezed raw fruit and vegetable juices. This cleanses out much of your internal wastes so the super-charging effects of the minerals and enzymes in the desiccated liver and brewer's yeast will then be more concentrated upon your liver and not be sidetracked by having to cleanse out other portions of your body.

Your Liver Health Plan

1. Your liver is an internal sieve, a built-in filter which must process fats, sugars, starches, etc. Keep it clean with periodic controlled fasting to prevent the accumulation of toxic wastes and poisons.
2. Your liver stores iron, neutralizes toxic wastes, keeps your blood healthy and poison-free.
3. To keep a clean liver, *eliminate* refined foods, sugars, starches from a refined source, coffee, tea, excitants, sharp condiments, excessive animal fat intake.
4. Try the desiccated liver-brewer's yeast combo in the One-Day Liver-Clean controlled fasting plan.

15

Better Tooth Health Through Controlled Fasting

Is it possible to reduce incidence of tooth decay by means of controlled fasting? The answer is a hopeful yes. In fact, by means of elimination of certain harmful foods, you can strengthen the tooth enamel to the point where cavities may be a rare situation. Certain foods and beverages have been seen to deposit a waste residue on the teeth, leaving toxic substances that actually "burn" into the enamel and tooth structure. This happens to youngsters as well as oldsters. I mention this because most of you regard tooth loss with advanced years.

According to the American Dental Association, it is estimated that over 50 million Americans of all ages wear artificial teeth of one kind or another. By the age of 35, two out of three adults need replacements for one or more of their natural teeth. Another expert says that 24 out of every 25 youngsters are being successfully attacked yearly by toxic substances that cause dental cavities *even before they reach school age!*

Few of you have "perfect teeth." By the age of 30, the average American has about 12 healthy, unfilled teeth. The rest (what are left of the original 32) are either missing, capped, filled or have been substituted for. Also, 15 out of every 100 Americans have dentures; another 20 out of 100 could use them but for various reasons do not have them.

HEALTHY TEETH

Under normal conditions of proper diet, a full set of adult teeth should be a healthy 32; there are 16 each in the upper and lower jaws. The *crown* of a tooth is that portion seen above the gum line; it is only about 1/3 of the whole tooth. Beneath the gum line lie the *roots*. The crown of each tooth is covered with dental *enamel*, the hardest body substance. The roots are encased in *cementum*, not quite as hard. Inside the enamel and cementum is the rather softer bony substance known as *dentin* which comprises the bulk of the tooth. The dentin surrounds a *pulp chamber* in which are found the tooth's nerves and blood vessels. These nerves and blood vessels run up and down through slender channels called *root canals*, through which they connect with the rest of the circulatory and body nervous systems. Covering the roots of the tooth is the *periodontal membrane* which holds the tooth in the jaw socket, absorbs some of the chewing shock. That's why teeth are slightly movable.

TOXIC WASTES

The very foundation of tooth decay or mouth disorders is in the accumulation of toxic wastes as we shall presently see. These wastes (lactobacillus acidophilus) and also lactic acid, dissolve the enamel or outer structure of the tooth and pour through the tiniest breaks. Once through the enamel, the toxic waste eats at the dentin, destroying the mineral content. The tooth now becomes sensitive to heat, cold or sweets because of this tiny hole or cavity. Gradually, the wastes eat into more of the enamel until a larger cavity results, ' approaching the pulp chamber, irritating the nerves and a toothache starts.

Of course, tooth decay may be repaired with a filling; but toxemia may strike at the root canals. There may be an accumulation of the toxic waste known as tartar or dental calculus and this is more serious.

Mouth disorders occur because of toxemia. Pyorrhea consists of inflammation and degeneration of the periodontal membranes that surround each tooth. (Did you know that this is the most common cause of tooth loss after age 35?) Pyorrhea is sparked by the ravaging and destructive effects of mouth bacteria or toxic wastes and poisonous substances. There is also *gingivitis* or bleeding gums; this consists of loss or recession of the bony structure that supports the teeth in their sockets. Consequently, teeth become loose and may fall out. Toxic wastes can destroy precious skin and cellular connective tissues in the gums. Proper mouth hygiene is essential to tooth health. In addition, the mouth bacteria and poisonous substances that lead to tooth decay must be neutralized and washed out of the system.

HOW AN ACTRESS BUILT UP THE NATURAL BEAUTY OF HER TEETH

A film actress became worried about her teeth. "There's no such thing as makeup for teeth," she told me. "I've got stains on my front teeth that just won't come off. I've got more and more cavities. I don't want to bother having my teeth capped like so many others do in the theatrical profession. It's expensive and takes a long time. I wish I knew what I could do."

We were sitting in a small restaurant close to the Broadway theatrical district. "I'll tell you about a special 'tooth food' that I try. You see," was my explanation, "I was *born* with a tooth problem. I've got a condition known as malocclusion — an uneven bite. That means that whenever I chew food, my teeth are subjected to this uneven pressure. Impacted waste residues are more probable in people who have this condition, such as myself. So I manage to keep down tooth decay and have healthy teeth because of a special 'tooth food.' It's surprisingly simple."

She was all ears. "Tell me where to get it. I'll pay anything."

I snapped fingers to signal the waiter. "Fetch me one fresh, raw apple."

Moments later, the actress was eating the apple as I explained, "That's all there is to it. You see, apples are powerfully rich in potassium — a mineral that is able to neutralize the harmful effects of mouth toxins and waste substances that become lodged to the teeth and in the crevices and nooks of the gums. The potassium in the apple helps fight bacteria, combats the harmful effects of virus infections, washes the bloodstream and rejuvenates the cells and tissues — and that includes the same cells and tissues in your mouth — potassium is like a detergent. That's it, the mineral attacks the dirt that has encrusted the teeth and gums, detoxifies the harmful bacteria, leaving your mouth fresh and clean. If you want to help turn your teeth into pearls of beauty — try potassium in a simple, fresh apple."

The actress tried this plan — and also utilized a surprisingly simple controlled fasting method and later went on to the bigger and better things in show business. In fact, I hear that her radiant smile is regarded as the most natural and healthful in show business.

Many dentists, as well as Fred D. Miller, D.D.S., author of *Open Door to Health,* have found that tooth decay and toxic waste can be kept to a minimum by means of using an apple — *Nature's toothbrush* — after each meal. That is, you wash and pare a whole apple (preferably one that is organically grown and free from harmful effects of insecticides and sprays) and eat it after each meal. Chew thoroughly so the potassium is liberated and sent to wash out the accumulated toxic debris.

YOUR CONTROLLED FASTING TOOTH HEALTH PLAN

Here are the causes of tooth decay and the harmful foods that introduce a slough of debris and toxic wastes into the mouth and system. Learn to eliminate these items from your fare and enjoy better tooth health.

1. *Refined sugars and refined starches.* Mouth digestion of sugars and starches release harmful irritants that set up a condition of toxemia. These harmful bacterial substances eat into the enamel of your teeth, leading to decay. Eliminate all refined sugars, starches, carbohydrates. No cakes, no candies, no pastries, no pies, no sugary-syrups or foods containing them. Substitute with natural sweetening agents such as honey, raw brown sugar, etc., but in moderation!

2. *Soft drinks.* Toxic wastes are left on the enamel of teeth to cause erosion. In nearly all soft drinks there are certain ingredients that cause the erosion of the enamel and dentine. The average cola drink has a pH of about 2.6 which means it is very acid. This acid

is another name for a toxic waste. Avoid carbonated beverages. *Consumer Reports* advises: "The safest procedure is to minimize the risk of acid erosion by going easy with the more acid beverages, drinking them in moderation and preferably with food (which dilutes the acid effect)." Frankly, you will do best to avoid these carbonated drinks.

3. *Refined foods.* Most of these are treated with artificial substances that release a store of carbohydrates which, in turn, are transformed and leave a deposit of waste residue upon the teeth. These toxic substances are corrosive in the sense that they burn into the enamel and pave the way for tooth and mouth ailments.

Bearing these points out, we note that Dr. N. E. Goldsworthy reported to the *Medical Journal of Australia* that he was able to reduce and even eliminate tooth decay in youngsters by following this plan:

1. No white sugar, no white flour products. Refined starches were absent from the diet of the experimental youngsters.
2. Raw fresh vegetables were used extensively. The daily menu consists largely of nuts, dried fruits, fresh fruits, fruit juices and vitamin preparations.
3. Meals were eaten at regular, specified times and there was no between-meal snacking.

Dr. Goldsworthy says this: ". . . we can state unequivocally that abstention from refined carbohydrates is significantly associated with the maintenance of decay-free teeth. It will be objected that the white flour and sugar and their products are necessary, if not dietetically, then at least economically, because these items are the cheapest components of our food. However, the wealth of this favored nation, if wisely used, could easily provide the alternative types of diet . . . Despite the cherished belief that calories or energy can be obtained only from sugary food, there is no evidence that refined carbohydrates are essential to good health."

Natural foods, by the way give good energy. Any naturally sweet food with sugar — pears, corn, watermelons, prunes, dates, apples — provide heathful energy.

Toxic acids are waste by-products of white flour and white sugar that tend to break down tooth enamel and lead to decay, also they saturate the bloodstream and other vital fluids surrounding the cells of the teeth and gums. Controlled fasting requires elimination of these foods as an essential step in building a healthy mouth and strengthening the teeth.

TOOTH BRUSHING TIPS

Clean out toxic wastes with good brushing. Use a brush made with natural bristles rather than nylon or artificial or synthetic bristles because the latter scratch and irritate the mouth. Here are six ways to help brush away debris and toxic wastes:

1. Begin with a completely dry brush. Before you brush, finger-massage your gums. Place bristles of the brush flat against the teeth, the bristles being parallel to the teeth and pointing toward the gums. Move the handle from side to side so the bristles bend, and keep up regularly.

2. Do not scrub your gums. The bristle ends should not move from their original position when the brush is pumped — not moved.

3. When you brush the front of your lower front teeth, hold your lip away to prevent injury to it.

4. If bothered with bleeding gums, keep your lip away and also keep your brush away from your gums.

5. You brush by turning the brush to an angle of 45° by twisting the handle until the outer row of bristles touches the gums, creating sufficient pressure to bend the bristles.

6. Doing as described above, your gums will turn a little pale under the pressure because debris-laden blood is sent out and the stagnant pools of toxic wastes are being liberated and now fresh blood is sent to the gums.

Your teeth should remain strong and healthy with proper diet and controlled fasting — that is, elimination of refined foods. A mouthful of healthy teeth is a sign of youth and good looks. There is nothing like good teeth to really make you feel and look the picture of health. Pearly white teeth are possible with controlled fasting.

Tooth Saving Tips of This Chapter

1. Toxic wastes are left by refined starches, sweets, carbohydrates, soft drinks. Controlled fasting calls for elimination of these so-called foods.

2. The potassium in a fresh, organically grown apple can nullify the poisonous effects of toxic bacteria in the mouth and on the teeth. Eat a fresh apple every day.

3. Eliminate refined sugars and refined starches, soft drinks, refined foods — substitute with natural foods for better tooth and gum health.

16

Controlled Fasting, the One Best Way to Stop the Alcohol Drinking Habit

Drinking and alcoholism can be traced to an uncontrollable urge from within; that urge is sparked by certain irritants present in the bloodstream, the same type of debris and accumulation of waste materials that set up internal chain reactions to undermine overall body and mind health. Just as a cinder in your eye creates total discomfort, the presence of foreign and unwanted substances in your bloodstream create a nagging desire to "do something" that usually leads to the urge to drink alcoholic beverages.

MacCallum's *Textbook of Pathology* declares that alcohol is "the commonest of poisons that affect human beings and that protracted habitual use seems to give rise to many anatomical changes in the organs." Waste substances left by alcohol infests vital body organs to create a condition of internal toxemia.

Henry H. Rusby, M.D., in *Reference Handbook of the Medical Sciences,* also asserts that the effects of alcohol are like "those of a drug which for a very brief period stimulates, then depresses the tissues upon which it acts." It is "wholly depressing" upon the nervous system, infects the powers of mental vigor, the delicate functions of coordination, injures the liver, is often traced to Bright's disease (a form of inflammation of the kidneys), sets up toxic reactions to impair the function of the heart and blood circulation.

ALCOHOLISM AS A DISEASE

Alcoholism is regarded as a disease of toxemia, that is, alcohol passes directly into the bloodstream from the stomach within an hour of ingestion (the entry of most foods is delayed for several hours). Substances in the alcohol remain in the bloodstream to create infectious waste residues. The liver, through which alcohol is processed, receives many other waste residues leading to hardening and hepatitis and cirrhosis diseases. Alcohol deposits these wastes upon the liver and within its sieve-like tissues.

Alcoholism ranks among the major national health threats, along with cancer, mental illness and heart disease.

There are some 80 million people who drink, in our country. Many are unharmed because of moderation. But to an estimated 6½ million, drinking has become enough of a problem to interfere with a healthy life. These are alcoholics — victims of a debris-laden bloodstream and toxic-infected body.

DESTRUCTIVE EFFECTS

Toxic wastes in alcohol enter the bloodstream to create destructive effects; these residues anesthetize the control mechanism in the brain, nullify the thinking processes, set up an internal upheaval. Alcohol followed by or taken with water will move into the bloodstream slower than when it is consumed with soda water because carbon dioxide shoots toxemia into the system, taking along the liquor.

Toxic wastes are carried by the bloodstream to the neurons of the cerebral cortex of the brain to infect the delicate tissues, to create a corrosive effect. This may lead to headaches, a dilation of the blood vessels, nausea (as the body struggles to give off the waste substances), vertigo, exhaustion, tension, etc. A higher concentration of liquor, 100 proof or more, sends more toxic wastes to the stomach mucosa, invites secretion of mucus in an attempt by the body to render some self-protection. It does not really work and succeeds only in delaying the eventual consequences.

In nearly every group of 30 or more people, there is usually one alcoholic. That alcoholic may be male or female.

HOW AN ALCOHOLIC WOMAN LOST OUT

A young woman was addicted to that 5 o'clock drink, at first. Susan was a librarian, had a good educational background, wanted to mix in with the after-hours crowd. At first, she took the evening drink and went home. Soon, she started on a bar-hopping round that ended in nightly drinking bouts. "But I'm sober in the morning," she insisted. "I still go to work." Yet, as she progressed in the drinking stages, she began to fade. She wasted away. Debris-laden alcohol started to "devour" the millions of delicate body tissues and she looked much older than her 29. "What can I do?" she lamented when she could no longer concentrate on her job and was in jeopardy of being dismissed. "I never thought I'd be an alcoholic."

I explained about the fasting method as a means of ridding the body of poisons. "I know that you're no longer hungry because drinking has supplanted the desire for food. But controlled fasting is *not* elimination of food. It is a special plan designed to remove offending substances from the body, chronic irritants that spark the urge to drink."

Bleary-eyed, weak, nervous and pale, Susan agreed to follow a special controlled fasting plan — based upon the understanding that the alcoholic's body has a chronic inability to handle carbohydrates properly and that is the reason why alcohol spells doom. Carbohydrates and starches leave residue and waste materials that cannot be properly metabolized, setting up a condition of internal toxemia that attacks vital body organs including the hypo-adrenocortical function affecting the mind.

In this special controlled fasting diet, aimed at cleansing the bloodstream and easing the carbohydrate metabolization function, alcoholism can be conquered as complete as you may want it. Susan tried this diet for a period of three weeks — and it worked for her. She licked the compulsive drinking habit! (I'll give you this controlled fasting system in a little while.)

Two months later, when I returned to the library for further research on a nutrition matter, I saw Susan as she was being led through a rear door, out into the street, into a cab. I say "led" because she was staggering, she was bleary-eyed, looked a mess. I asked a co-worker about the problem. The co-worker told me that Susan had refrained from alcohol because she followed a special diet plan — but she lost self-control, returned to foolish eating and began to slide down again. Unhappily, her career is ended. And she was the one who declared, "Who me?" when it was suggested that a 5 o'clock cocktail could lead to a drinking problem.

ALCOHOL CAUSES TOXEMIA

Understand this — in a condition of diabetes, carbohydrates cannot be properly metabolized because of insufficient secretion of insulin from the pancreatic gland; insulin is supposed to metabolize carbohydrates. The patient suffers from *high* blood sugar. Now, in the case of alcoholism, there is *too much insulin* being secreted by the pancreas with the result that the alcoholic has *low* blood sugar. In controlled fasting, the excessive insulin needs to be drained off.

How and why? The function of these two glands is involved: the *adrenals* (and it is the cortex or covering of the gland that must remain free of toxemia, particularly) and the *pituitary* which regulates the adrenals. These two glands must be kept free of waste materials by means of controlled fasting. The special diet will be given to you presently, just bear with me a page or two more.

E. M. Abrahamson, M.D., in *Body, Mind and Sugar,* tells us,

> Alcoholism is caused by a deficiency in the adrenal cortical hormones — those hormones whose action is antithetical to insulin. The trouble may not be in the adrenal cortical itself, however, but in the master gland, the pituitary, which for some reason fails to stimulate the adrenal cortical glands as it does in normal operation of the endocrine system. It is believed, moreover, that this disability of the pituitary is not caused by the alcoholism itself but antedates its development.

The alcohol deposits waste residues and toxic refuse upon the glands which suffer from impaired function. Alcoholism is traced to a condition of hyperinsulinism with a chronic partial blood sugar starvation because these glands (adrenals and pituitary) are infested with wastes.

THE CARBOHYDRATE MENACE

Carbohydrates or starches are quick energy sources. The alcoholic feels depressed and eats carbohydrate foods for a quick lift. This introduces more toxemia into the system. Refined sugar and starch foods become internally fermented to create a condition similar to alcoholic ingestion by means of tissue-saturation with waste residues. A reduction in carbohydrate and sugar foods will help give the body a chance to self-cleanse itself.

You must stick to the plan if you expect it to succeed. In Susan's case, it worked until she started to slide and began to eat taboo foods and introduced irritants into her blood system which, in turn, tempted her to reach for a drink.

The following is a controlled fast for controlling low blood sugar, which, in turn, leads to internal cleanliness. The obvious benefit is mastering the alcohol habit.

INTERNAL CLEANSING FOR CONTROLLING THE CRAVING FOR ALCOHOL

On Arising — Medium orange, half grapefruit or four ounces of fruit juice.

Breakfast — Fruit or 4 ounces of juice, 1 egg with or without 2 slices of ham or bacon; only one slice of bread or toast with plenty of butter, beverage.

2 Hours after breakfast — 4 ounces of juice.

Lunch — Meat, fish, cheese or eggs; salad (large serving of lettuce, tomato or Waldorf salad with mayonnaise or French dressing); vegetables if desired; only one slice of bread or toast with plenty of butter; dessert; beverage.

3 Hours after lunch — 8 ounces of milk.

1 Hour before dinner — 4 ounces of juice.

Dinner — Soup, if desired (not thickened with flour); vegetables; liberal portion of meat, fish or poultry; only one slice of bread if desired; dessert; beverage.

2-3 Hours after dinner — 8 ounces of milk.

Every 2 hours until bedtime — 4 ounces of milk or a small handful of nuts.

Allowable Vegetables: Asparagus, avocado, beets, broccoli, Brussels sprouts, cabbage, cauliflower, carrots, celery, cucumbers, corn, eggplant, lima beans, onions, peas, radishes, sauerkraut, squash, string beans, tomatoes, turnips.

Allowable Fruits: Apples, apricots, berries, grapefruit, pears, melons, oranges, peaches, pineapple, tangerines. May be cooked or raw, with or without cream but without sugar. Canned fruits should be packed in water, not syrup. Lettuce, mushrooms and nuts may be taken as freely as desired.

Juice: Any unsweetened fruit or vegetable juice except grape or prune juice.

Beverages: Weak tea (tea ball not brewed); decaffeinated coffee, coffee substitutes.

Desserts: Fruit, unsweetened gelatin, junket (made from tablets, not mix).

Soft Drinks: Club soda, dry ginger ale.

AVOID ABSOLUTELY

Sugar, candy and other sweets, such as cake, pie, pastries, sweet custards, puddings and ice cream.

Caffeine: Ordinary coffee, strong brewed tea, beverages containing caffeine. (Your doctor will tell you what these are.)

Potatoes, rice, grapes, raisins, plums, figs, dates and bananas should be avoided while on the alcoholic-recuperative program.

Spaghetti, macaroni and noodles; also avoid crackers, biscuits, pretzels and starch-containing snacks.

Wines, cordials, cocktails and beer.

ALSO

It would be wise to omit bacon, ham, soft drinks because these contain artificial stimulants, spices, etc., which leave toxic wastes in the bloodstream.

The above internal cleansing plan has been seen to work in normalizing blood sugar and cleansing the system of waste residues left by sugars and starches.

CAN DRINKING BE SAFE?

Frankly, once internal toxemia has taken over and tissue-ravaging commences, the vicious cycle is anything but safe. However, many have asked me to find a so-called safe way to drink. There is *no* such safe way. You cannot bargain with a clean inside condition. But a way to help prevent chronic alcoholism is proposed by William B. Terhune, M.D., director of the Silver Hill Foundation of New Canaan, Connecticut as reported to *Science News Letter.* Here are his 10 steps:

1. Never take a drink when you "need one."
2. Sip slowly and space your drinks. Take a second drink 30 minutes after the first, the third an hour after the second. Never a fourth drink.
3. Dilute your alcohol.
4. Keep an accurate and truthful record of the amount and number of drinks you take — never take a drink every day.
5. Do not drink on an empty stomach.
6. Never conceal the amount of alcohol you drink. Instead, exaggerate it.
7. Stop drinking on "signal" such as lunch, dinner, fatigue, sex stimulation, boredom, frustration and bedtime.
8. When tired or tense, soak in a hot tub and follow with a cold shower.
9. Make it a rule never to take a drink to escape discomfort — either physical or mental.
10. Never, never take a drink in the morning thinking it will offset a hangover.

Those of you who find it difficult to lick the drinking problem with controlled fasting should start a slow abatement of drink based upon the preceding 10-point plan until your will power is strong enough to go to the controlled fasting plan.

A SPECIAL CURE FOR ALCOHOLISM

Dr. Alice Chase who has her own clinic in upstate New York, noted author of *Nutrition for Health,* cured a young patient of alcoholism by means of a special controlled fasting plan as follows:

1. She was put to bed on rest cure (the patient, that is), for a period

of three days during which time the food intake consisted of freshly squeezed orange juice, grapefruit juice and lemonade — the latter sweetened with honey. These beverages were given to the alcoholic at two-hour intervals. At her bedside table, the patient had one or two glasses of fruit juice with an ice cube or two in it. The "secret" here is that the cold drink serves as a substitute to satisfy the craving for liquor.

2. The bowels were cleansed once or twice a day by means of an enema to get rid of toxic wastes.

3. On the fourth day, the diet changed:

   Breakfast — an egg, slice of toast, glass of Postum, small dish of cereal with sweet cream. She could eat fresh raw fruit at any time.

   Luncheon — steamed vegetable, baked potato or rice, glass of raw vegetable juice.

   Dinner — raw salad with cottage cheese or any other kind of natural cheese that was unprocessed, steamed vegetables, glass of fresh fruit juice, glass of milk or buttermilk.

Within two weeks of this controlled fasting plan, the patient succeeded in ending the drinking urge, cleansing her insides and was now energetic, emotionally robust and cheerful. Four weeks later, she was like a new person. At the same time, it was advised that she be removed from any environment that may be tempting her to drink.

SERIOUS PROBLEM

Yes, it *is* a serious problem — industry and taxpayers are charged one billion dollars yearly traced to accidents, absenteeism, production loss, premature medical disabilities. Alcoholism is responsible for more broken homes, more crime, more juvenile delinquency than any other cause. Directly or adversely, alcoholism affects at least four other individuals for every person afflicted — a total of 20 million people, nearly one-ninth of our population. If you are a drinker or want to help a drinker, you cannot ignore the problem. You may respond to the method of internal cleansing and controlled fasting as it has helped so many others.

Suppose the alcoholic wants outside help also. The following organizations may be of service:

1. ALCOHOLICS ANONYMOUS, P. O. Box 459, Grand Central Station, New York, N.Y. 10017. Find a listing for AA in your local telephone directory or write to them for information. This group is an informal fellowship of those who have "learned the hard way" by personal experience. They help themselves and others by means of a recovery program based on 12 steps. They'll give you this program if you contact them. I have the program here but success depends upon *you* getting the program yourself so I'll not interfere.

2. AL-ANON FAMILY GROUPS COUNCIL, 125 East 23rd Street, New York, N.Y. 10010. Many communities have such groups who get together and help one another with common problems. Write to the office for information about a group closest to your home.

3. NATIONAL COUNCIL ON ALCOHOLISM, INC. Two East 103rd Street, New York, N.Y. 10029. An information center that will send you pamphlets and books. They have established local affiliated councils in about 60 cities operating many Alcoholism Information Centers that offer you educational material, personal consultation and referral to best resources for individual needs.

4. HEALTH DEPARTMENTS. Ask at any local hospital for the name and address of your nearest state and local health department. Many have facilities for the study and treatment of alcoholism and can help you.

Please note that alcoholism takes time to develop; the internal toxemia condition is not an overnight condition. Therefore, recovery and internal cleansing under controlled fasting takes time, too. Patience and understanding is needed. The problem can be solved. Look to controlled fasting as the answer to the control of the alcohol drinking habit.

Your Stop-Drinking Plan

1. Cleanse your bloodstream, normalize your blood sugar, restrict sugars and starches and carbohydrate intake.
2. Follow the "Internal Cleansing Diet" for a period of 30 days as a means of cleansing the wastes out of your system.
3. If it's difficult, try the 10-step "safe drinking" plan to flush out some of the wastes from your body and strengthen resistance.
4. Follow the 3-step plan as per Dr. Alice Chase's recommendation.
5. Seek aid from outside sources such as the associations listed at the end of this chapter. They are ready to help you — *if* you want to be helped. If you do *not* want to be helped, forget all that you have read in this chapter!

17

How Controlled Fasting Can Give You Youthful and Beautiful Skin

Lovely to look at . . . beautiful to see . . . how youthful you look . . . such a picture of health . . . a complexion of peaches and cream . . . milk and honey . . .

Flattery? Perhaps. Justified? Your mirror can tell you. A toxic-free body will give a clear skin, rosy cheeks, free from blemishes and premature aging symptoms. Yet, there are many who have such debris-laden insides, they have a sallow skin, blotches, shadows, a wan and tired look, pimples, acne, wrinkles, etc. A youthful and healthy skin is a reward for a clean inside body.

WHAT IS YOUR SKIN?

Actually, your skin is the largest organ of your body. It has an area of about 17 square feet on the average adult. It weighs about 6 pounds, twice as heavy as your liver or brain. Your skin receives one-third of all blood circulating in your body so a debris-laden blood means a debris-filled skin. Also, your skin has from 2 to 3 million sweat glands (especially abundant in the armpits, on the hands and feet and forehead). The average adult has over 3,000 square inches of surface area. Thickness varies from about 1/50 of an inch on your eyelids to as high as 1/3 of an inch on palms and soles.

Your skin protects your body against bacterial invasion, against injury to sensitive tissues within your body, against harsh sunshine rays and also against loss of needed moisture.

Your skin serves as an organ of perception for the entire nervous system. If you examine just *one* square inch of skin under a microscope, you'd discover 72 feet of nerves, hundreds of pain, pressure, heat and cold receptors. Your skin also regulates temperature.

That same square inch of skin alone contains about 15 feet of blood vessels which grow larger (dilate) when your body needs to lose heat. And these same vessels narrow (constrict) when your body needs to retain heat loss through the skin. And all of these 72 feet of nerves, receptors, etc., are found in just one square inch of skin!

SKIN MAKEUP

No, I'm not referring to the makeup worn by the females, but the internal makeup that really determines beauty and health and youth. Your skin is made up of three tissue layers: epidermis, dermis and subcutaneous. The *epidermis* or outer skin consists of two layers — the horny top layer of dry dead cells constantly being shed, and the growing layer which constantly replaces dead cells with new cells. The deeper layers of the epidermis form new cells.

The *dermis* layer, often called the "true skin" contains the nerves, sweat glands, blood vessels, nerve receptors, hair follicles, oil glands. The top of the dermis contains a layer of tiny cone-shaped objects called papillae — over 150 million papillae are scattered over the entire body. More are found in sensitive areas such as fingertips. Nerve fibers and special nerve endings are found in many papillae which gives you a sense of touch and "feel" as well as response to being touched.

The *subcutaneous* layer contains fat lobules, blood vessels and serves as a smooth and springy base for the skin. It links the dermis (middle layer) with tissue covering the muscles and bones.

COMMON SKIN PROBLEMS

Internal debris has been seen to blame for many common skin problems. *Acne* is a condition in which certain hormones react by forcing the skin's oil glands (sebaceous glands) into powerful action to send toxic wastes through the skin pores and out of the body. The pores become clogged by surface dirt; a mild infection erupts into an acne pimple. *Wrinkles* or *crow's feet* occur when excessive toxemia disturbs the sebaceous glands. This process reduces the working skin layers to a small fraction of their former thickness, topped by an outer layer that is harder and thicker, resulting in accentuation of lines and wrinkles. Toxemia also increases manufacture of melanin, the brownish pigment that gives a natural color to the skin; excessive melanin causes darkening of the skin and may indicate a need to cleanse the insides of internal toxemia and debris.

Flakes on the skin and scalp know as *dandruff* are likewise traced to Nature's effort to rid your body of internal wastes. Dandruff is caused when your glands attempt to slough off wastes via the pores by means of *sebum* (fatty or oily secretions of the sebaceous glands). An excess of waste-laden sebum on your scalp causes dandruff — tiny flecks of dead skin "glued" together.

WASHING TIP

Your skin has a slight (but natural) acid content. Most soaps are highly alkaline and will wash away the protective acid coating. To help keep your skin more acid, rinse your face and hands in a basin of water to which has been added the juice of one lemon. After washing and drying with a towel, squeeze a few drops of lemon juice on your hands and rub palms together. You might even rub your face with the cut half of a lemon to restore the natural acid condition.

CONTROLLED FASTING

Cleansed insides means cleansed oil glands that secrete normal sebum that is free from toxic wastes. To begin, here are some suggestions for cleansing your insides, according to J. DeWitt Fox,

M.D., in *Life and Health* (Vol. 73, No. 1): "Besides the tendency to omit the bathroom scrub up, a teen-age weakness is the after-school snack or ice cream soda stop on the way home. To side-step acne, sweets are taboo! In place of heavy fats and sweets, let Johnny and Sally enjoy the social hour with their friends sipping a refreshing fruit drink."

Avoid chocolates! Dr. Fox says, "Chocolate, a pleasant flavoring for many sweets, is perhaps the worse enemy, for chocolate contains a heavy hard-to-digest fat. This fat — cocoa butter — eaten in large quantities accumulates in the skin, to clog the pores and cause blackheads pimples and disfiguring skin blemishes."

What about vitamins? Two nutrients should be emphasized: the first, Vitamin A, the skin vitamin, can be obtained in such delicious foods as yellow squash, pumpkin, carrots, apricots, green leafy vegetables and red beets — the yellow, green and red vegetables — sometimes it must be taken in capsule form during the wintertime."

The second vitamin is Vitamin D — the sunshine vitamin — important for strong teeth and bones, steady nerves and normal calcium metabolism — is actually manufactured in your skin when you get your share of sunshine.

If we want to cleanse our insides and free ourselves of internal toxemia, get out in the fresh air and sunshine. Clothing should not be too tight nor chafe at the skin which leads to infections and irritations.

Incidentally, food supplements and capsules of vitamins are sold at pharmacies and health food stores.

IMPORTANCE OF IMPROVED CIRCULATION

Stagnant pools of toxic-laden blood means that circulation has to be improved. Free your insides from these pockets of sludge and slime and sources of infectious wastes. Dr. Fox suggests that before you go to bed, fill your bathtub with hot water, sit on the edge, insert both feet into the tub "until they are lobster red." Then fill the tub with warm water, get in and relax yourself. Then get out, wrap up in a big towel. Anoint your skin with a light oil, hop into bed. This keeps your circulation moving.

The following morning, turn on the shower to a comfortable

warmth. Step in. When you are nice and warm all over, switch to a cooler shower. Do this three times — alternately hot and cold, ending with the cold. Jump out, then rub briskly with a towel. Feel your skin tingle and glow with vitality? Good! It means that the blood is circulating and wastes are being sent to the pores to be given off.

INTERNAL CLEANSING PLAN

1. Daily, eat a portion of fat-trimmed meat (or fish or vegetable plate) as well as fresh raw fruit and vegetables; try to get those that are organically grown. Sprays and insecticides introduce wastes and toxic residues in your system so be careful as possible to get organically grown foods. Avoid fats that become solid at room temperature since they interfere with normal glandular function and clog up the hormonal system.
2. Shun frozen dinners, prepared meat pies, cake mixes, so-called "convenience" foods, devitalized breads, etc. These are all possibly treated with chemicals that create internal toxemia.
3. Sensible exposure to fresh air and sunshine, movement is a good skin tonic. Skin cells require stimulation so try a 30 to 60 minute walk in a fresh air region such as a park or by the seaside or in the woods, daily.
4. Remember the essential unsaturated fatty acids which help dry skin become soft and velvety. Add just one tablespoonful of unprocessed wheat germ, peanut oil or soybean oil to your raw vegetable salads.
5. Minerals are good, too. Want your skin to glow? You can have this when iron-rich red blood pours through strong capillaries and healthy blood vessels. Iron is found in blackstrap molasses, apricots, leafy greens. How can you cleanse your bloodstream, keep it from becoming sluggish and slow? Bathe your skin cells in healthy and toxic-free blood. Remember the leafy greens. Try iodine in capsule form sold at pharmacies and health stores.

In the words of a wise doctor, you have a fascinating skin. And if you take good care of it, it will keep you looking young and beautiful for a long time. True skin beauty means good health. Beauty from within is the only kind that is more than skin deep.

PUFFY EYES

Toxic wastes in the capillaries leading to the eyes are trying to get out. Here's a method of relief for puffy eyes that may also be swollen and inflamed. Bathe the eyes with warm witch hazel or warm boric acid solution. Follow at once with a bath of cold boric acid or cold witch hazel. The warm solution relaxes the skin, soothes the inflammation. The cold solution relieves the puffiness, tightens the skin.

CORN MEAL BATH

Your skin wants to get rid of 30% of body waste daily and take in 60% of oxygen. The pores must be clean and healthy to accomplish such a task. Here's a folk remedy you might try. Fill a tub with water. Before you get in, wet your body with a wash cloth. Pour a tablespoon of coarse ground corn meal into the palm of your hand and rub over your wet body until the meal is gone. It will not foam nor will it wear out your skin. Repeat until you've covered all areas. Now, step into the tub and soak. Glide your hands over your skin and you'll experience a silky feeling and a wonderfully vibrant reaction. Your skin breathes! After 30 minutes of soaking, take a 5 minute lukewarm shower, towel yourself and enjoy a healthy, glowing skin that is free of toxic wastes.

A QUEEN'S TONIC

An English Queen's skin beauty secret (in addition to the moist climate of England) is barley water. She drinks several glasses daily, as do the rest of her royal family. Possibly, the toxic wastes are flushed out of the system and this leads to a healthy skin. The royal family does have enviably young skin. Here's the tonic:

½ cup pearl barley

2½ quarts boiling water

2 lemons

6 oranges, unsprayed variety

Brown or raw sugar (or honey) to taste

Squeeze the lemons and oranges, saving both the juice and the rinds. Put barley in a large kettle. Add boiling water and cover. Simmer for 60 minutes. Strain water from the barley into a pitcher; add rinds of one lemon and three oranges. Add honey or sugar and let stand till cold. Remove rinds. Add juice of lemons and oranges and refrigerate.

You, too, may be a queen of beauty with this barley water drink because of its internal cleansing power.

WRINKLE CREAM

Ask your pharmacist to prepare this formula: $1\frac{1}{2}$ ounces lanolin; 5 drams petrolatum; 5 drams olive oil; 2 drams castor oil. Rub nightly on wrinkles. These ingredients are absorbed into the pores and serve to cleanse out the dead matter and excreta that may be responsible for the wrinkles.

To stimulate a sluggish and debris-laden skin, make a lotion of 1 ounce of boric acid in 2 ounces of witch hazel. Apply regularly to your skin. If possible, spend a weekend with this lotion on your skin. But maintain your controlled fasting plan consistently as well.

BLACKHEADS

Ask your pharmacist to prepare this formula: $1\frac{1}{2}$ ounces stearic acid, 15 drops triethanolamine; 3 ounces distilled water. Apply this cream to blackhead region every single night. It has helped many get rid of toxic wastes that erupt as blackheads.

FACIAL EXERCISES

In a word — *yawn!* This helps bring into play many muscles and also aids in ridding the facial area of stagnant pools of debris-laden blood. Also, place fingertips on cheekbones, pull your skin in all directions to revitalize them. And, place forefingers on temples, thumbs on jaw bone and move skin in all directions. This can aid a great deal in getting all the benefits from your fasting routines.

INSECT BITES

Did you know that mosquitoes and insects attack those who eat heavily of sugars and salts? It's a fact. Diabetics who must restrict sugar intake are known for being practically immune to insect bites, for the most part.

A young couple sent their little son to summer camp each year only to have him return with a body filled with blotches caused by mosquitoes and other woodsy insects. It reached the point where they were afraid to send him to camp and kept him home. What to do? I suggested they put him on a low-sugar fast — that is, *no sugar* added to foods nor sugar in cola drinks, cakes, confections, etc. All sugars were to be eliminated. Three months of a sugar-free diet and their son built a natural immunity so that when he was sent to summer camp, he just had a few usual bites. In fact, while other children suffered, he remained free from discomfort because he abstained from sugar in the camp and pushed away desserts and foods containing sugar. He was well-trained.

"We're on the same sugar-free plan," his parents told me, "and we're enjoying insect bite immunity, too."

Sugar is metabolized and transformed into waste residue into the system; the body seeks to dispose of this toxemia via the pores. Insects seem to sense this and attack the waste residue. Insects like sweets. That is a scientific fact! They thrive on sweets given off by your pores. The carbon dioxide combined with the toxic wastes that seep through your pores will attact these insects.

Other anti-insect tips: The *culex pipiens* or common household mosquito will shun you to a certain degree if you follow these tips:

1. Avoid colognes, after-shave lotions, perfumes. Insects are attracted to these.
2. Wear light clothing. Researchers at Union Carbide Corporation and entomologists at the University of Western Ontario, have found that mosquitoes are attracted to such colors as black, dark red and dark blue. They are less attracted to white, yellows and light greens.
3. Don't scratch if you get a bite. Whenever the skin is penetrated, by the bite or your nails, to scratch means that harmful bacteria can enter and infect. Wash with soap and water.

4. Prevent skin lesions with baking-soda solution, ammonia water, calamine lotions, rubbing alcohol.
5. My mother has a folk remedy that may have little scientific basis but it works for us — we eat a few garlic cloves whenever we have to go into an area which may cause mosquito bites. We enjoy immunity. Possibly because a substance in garlic is so volatile it offends insects (and humans, too) — or because garlic acts as an antiseptic in the bloodstream and makes us healthy. As stated before mosquitoes seem to thrive on wastes. That includes internal wastes that come through skin pores.
6. Soothe a bite by applying calamine lotion with 1% phenol added. Apply at the swelling region. Your pharmacist can prepare this lotion for you.

CONTROLLED FASTING SUGGESTIONS FOR SKIN HEALTH

ACNE

Best to avoid these foods — chocolate, nuts, pork, bacon, ham, cream, homogenized milk, butter, coffee, cocoa, greasy foods, gooey desserts, pastries and pies, fried foods, shellfish, iodized salt, cola and soft drinks, alcohol (all forms), sharp cheese, sugar.

SKIN LESIONS

Traced to the body's attempt to give off toxic wastes via the seborrhea glands. For clean sebum, avoid these foods: chocolate, cola and soft drinks, homogenized milk, gooey desserts, fried and greasy foods, spices, ham, cream, hot coffee, cocoa, tea, oily foods, bacon, iodized salt, bread, butter, excess potatoes, lobster, shrimp, cheeses that are spiced or creamy, pork. *Reduce intake* of salt, pepper, ketchup, mustard and condiments.

Remember to drink lots of freshly squeezed fruit and vegetable beverages to have a healthy bloodstream and a healthy skin. All the cosmetics in the world are useless if you have dirty insides! To have a youthful skin, clean out your insides first and then you'll bloom with radiant, waste-free delight.

Basic Points of This Chapter

1. Billions of pores in your skin are used as outlets to get rid of internal debris and waste substances. Keep your skin healthy so it can adequately slough off these toxic wastes.
2. Wash regularly. Try the controlled fasting plan and eliminate harmful foods.
3. Revitalize those stagnant pools of waste-laden blood in the body by proper bathing methods.
4. Go on a sugar-free fast for relief from insect bites.

18

Fomentations — the Secret of Internal Body Washing with Controlled Fasting

"I wish I were a sponge," lamented a tired, bedraggled and premature-aging bookkeeper. "That way, I could squeeze myself, get rid of all the unpleasant things inside of me." Her name was Janet and she was a bookkeeper-stenographer for an executive in a small department store in New York. "I just feel bloated up inside, and sickly. I hate to keep calling in for sick leave but there are days when I can barely drag myself off to work. If I were a sponge, I'd soak myself, then squeeze myself dry and clean."

"You've been reading too many science-fiction stories," was my comment. "I read of those humanoid sponges, too. Convenient, I agree. Human sponge-like creatures who jump in a pool, inflate themselves with water and then squeeze themselves like real sponges until all the inside wastes are flushed out."

"But they do feel wonderful when it's over with," Janet maintained, then sighed, "and I wish I could do the same for myself."

"You can! That's right. You *can* create the same sponge-clean effect on your body. It's no science-fiction fantasy but an actuality." That was my way of introducing Janet to an ancient "internal washing" method that revitalized such immortal health enthusiasts as Hippocrates, Plato, Socrates and others of the Golden Age of history. Janet tried this method during a spare evening, then embarked upon a regular "internal washing" plan every single night — and she so supercharged herself with cleanliness of mind and body, she made this plan a permanent fixture in her youthified life. You, too, can benefit by this ancient method of turning yourself into a sponge and washing out your unclean insides with the aid of controlled fasting.

FOMENTATIONS

The secret of internal washing is known as fomentations. This word is taken from the Greek-Latin derivative, *fomentum,* meaning "warm lotion" and this is precisely what it is. A fomentation is an application of warm, moist heat to a certain body part to relieve an ache or pain. When this moist heat is applied, changes take place in the blood circulation. Blood vessels dilate, nerves relax. The skin pores expand so that internal toxins and wastes that circulate in the bloodstream are able to be flushed out of the skin through these openings. The ancients knew of this secret method and it was used to cure a wide variety of ailments. Today, fomentations are gaining steady and increasing popularity because of the high rate of effectiveness.

In your quest for natural health *through controlled fasting,* do not overlook fomentations because when properly applied (details will be given you in this chapter), they can create a "sponge-like" effect on your body, bring to the skin surface many of the toxic wastes and pollutants that circulate in your system; the heat by means of its adhesive moist reaction will draw out these toxic irritants and cast them out of your body. The success of "sweat baths" is traced to this reaction; of course, steam baths and Turkish baths are rather exhausting to some. Furthermore, they treat the entire body as a whole while fomentations are highly concentrated in drawing out toxic wastes and internal debris from one specific joint or organ. The possibilities are limitless. While fomentations may be applied generally, they are particularly effective with *controlled fasting* to expel poisons from the body.

VARIOUS HELPS

J. Wayne McFarland, M.D., in *Life And Health* (Vol. LXXVII, No. 4), tells us that moist heat can be used in one of the simple home remedies for a variety of maladies. One of the best methods of applying moist heat to the body is with a fomentation. Regular fomentation cloths are much more effective than towels or ordinary cloths wrung from hot water and applied to the body because they hold the heat.

Fomentation treatments are one of the easiest ways of relaxing painful muscles that are in spasm, and so are helpful in treating rheumatism or arthritis. Muscular rheumatism, or fibrositis, is best treated by use of moist heat followed by massage and exercise."

The health benefits of moist heat are:

1. Neuritis and neuralgia pain responds with release of tension by means of fomentations.
2. Bursitis of the shoulder in the acute stage will be relieved by alternating ice packs with a set of fomentations. In more severe bursitis of the shoulder where the shoulder and arm are painfully stiff, fomentations should be applied to the site of pain, then followed with massage and exercise.
3. Acute back strain, lumbago as well as painful muscle spasm should be relieved with fomentation application.
4. Apply fomentations over the low back to relieve pain of kidney colic, from passing a kidney stone.
5. Lung inflammation (not due to tuberculosis) or severe bronchial disorders and sinus troubles will respond favorably to fomentations which are applied to the chest to alleviate soreness and tightness. The cough is lessened in severity because there is more blood going through the lung tissue than before the applications.
6. As for pneumonia, if it is traced to a virus, antibiotics may do no good and fomentations are a real benefit.

WHAT YOU WILL NEED

To make your fomentations, you will need the following: (1) Two sets of fomentation cloths. (2) Three towels. (3) A kettle of cold water and a washcloth. (4) An ample supply of boiling water. Keep the cloths and boiling water in the kitchen. The three towels, the kettle of cold water and washcloth are to be put at the bedside. The room in which this home treatment is given is to be free of cold drafts and comfortably warm, *not* chilly. You must be careful not to get chilled at any part of this home treatment.

HOW TO MAKE FOMENTATION CLOTHS

The most effective fomentation cloth is made from a 50% wool blanket. (A 100% wool blanket tends to shrink and become stiff when frequently heated.) Cut this blanket into three-foot squares. Prepare four of these squares. One will be used for the wet fomentation; the other will be used for a dry covering. Now, fold two of these squares into thirds for the wet portion so that you have two fomentation sets — there is an inside wet portion and an outside dry covering. That is, you will have two of these cloths that have been folded into a roll.

HOW TO HEAT FOMENTATION CLOTH

Hold the ends of one of these cloths; hold at both ends. Dip it into the boiling water until it is steaming hot. Let it soak, if necessary, but do not let go of the ends as you will not be able to stick your hands into the boiling water to retrieve the cloth and it should remain rolled up which is possible only if you hold tightly at the ends.

After the cloth is saturated with the boiling water, lift it up, twist it until all water possible is wrung out. Now, speedily untwist it. Place this steaming cloth on one of the dry cloths; rapidly you wrap this in the dry square which has a double thickness on the side which does not touch the wet cloth. Roll up the hot cloth in this dry cloth. Do this rapidly, but carefully, so the heat will be retained in the moist heat cloth.

HOW TO APPLY HEATED FOMENTATION

The body part that aches and is to receive this fomentation should be covered with the dry towel. Unroll the moist fomentation cloth over this towel and let it remain. The feeling of moist warmth now begins to spread over the affected region, stirring up the blood circulation, dilating arteries and veins and blood vessels, forcing stagnated pools of toxic debris and waste to start moving. The internal washing has begun.

If there is any feeling of irritation because of the heat, insert your hand under the dry towel, lift up and let the skin cool off for two moments. Then let the dry towel and the hot fomentation above, come down once again. Gradually, you should be able to endure more and more heat. I might add that the more heat you can *comfortably* and *safely* tolerate, the more effective is this remedy.

When the fomentation cloth begins to cool off, it is time to apply a new one. Usually, this takes about five minutes since the heat retained in the wool does not go beyond this time span.

As many as five such fomentation cloths can be applied to the afflicted area at one session. If you can have someone help you, so much the better. You can then remain in bed while your friend or family member applies the fomentation cloths which he will make himself, of course.

IN BETWEEN APPLICATIONS

Before removing the cooled off fomentation, rub the affected body part briskly with washcloth wrung dry from the kettle of cold water. After this cold application, dry the part thoroughly with a towel, place another towel (absolutely dry) over the area and now you are ready for the next fomentation application.

This cold application increases the flow of healthy and toxic-free blood to the affected part. When the skin glows a healthy pink, success is seen.

The ends of the hot fomentation cloth should be kept dry so the hands will not be burned while holding. After about five fomentation applications, end by a cold-washcloth rub or an alcohol rub to the part treated.

LARGE AREA TREATED

When fomentations are given to a large area such as the entire chest or abdomen, finish off with the alcohol rub or cold-towel rub to the *entire* body to prevent chilling; a good tip is to rub and dry each arm and leg individually to avoid a chill.

CHEST FOMENTATIONS

For any form of bronchial or respiratory congestion, directed to the chest, here are some suggestions: one fomentation is placed on the entire spine. The person should lie on his back (protect the bed with rubber sheeting or a bath towel) on top of this steaming fomentation — the cloth is not to touch the spinal column but has the towel in between to prevent burning — and the chest-up section is treated to fomentations at the same time. This is a double-fomentation that has worked wonders with many who suffer from sinus disorders, allergies, nasal sensitivities and colds, coughs, etc.

BETTER "SPONGE" POWER

Much of the secret power of fomentations lie in the sweating out of your internal wastes. To cause profuse sweating and turn yourself into a sponge to get rid of wastes inside the system, wrap fomentations around both of your feet and lower legs. You will have about four fomentations. At the same time, apply fomentations to your back or feet. When any of these fomentations get cool, change them. This over-all fomentation application will induce a healthy perspiration that will flush out toxic wastes from your pores.

As always, end a fomentation treatment with an alcohol rub or a cold-cloth rub; each part should then be thoroughly dried with a dry towel.

BRONCHITIS OR VIRUS PNEUMONIA

For these conditions, after the alcohol or cold-cloth rub, use cream, olive oil or powder to rub into the skin because this will close your pores more completely and give you greater protection against chilling.

For more involved applications, an ice cap or cold cloth to the forehead is helpful to prevent any feeling of weakness. This cloth should be changed frequently.

GENERAL PRECAUTIONS TO OBSERVE

Fomentations may be given to the very young and very aged, but they may be burned easily because of their sensitivity so be certain to wring the steaming wet fomentation cloth as dry as possible.

For those patients who have lost sensation in a certain body area under treatment, you should be doubly careful to avoid burns. These patients who have numb limbs — as in arthritis — may not feel extreme heat until a burn occurs. For such persons, the fomentations should be comfortably warm rather than very hot. As for cold applications, there is little chance of harm.

OTHER TIPS FOR SUCCESS

Remember to keep the room comfortably warm. If there is a chill or draft, the patient can be harmed. The most successful fomentation is possible when there is no chilling and the person's skin is a youthful pink — that is, the skin of the area that has been treated to the alternate hot and cold. Fomentations are helpful for those who suffer with aching, painful joints and muscular spasms.

8 BENEFITS OF FOMENTATIONS. There are many ailments that will respond to fomentations and here are the 8 most pronounced benefits when used during controlled fasting:

1. A chest cold will be relieved as will bronchial congestion.
2. Nervous disorders will be soothed, in particular when a fomentation is applied to the spine since this acts as a natural sedative.
3. Neuralgic pains are eased when wastes and debris are shifted by the moist heat action.
4. Arthritic pains are eased because infectious wastes are given off through dilated blood vessels and through the skin pores of the surrounding area of the painful joint.
5. The moist heat brings blood to the surface, thereby lessens pain of inflammation.
6. When used alternately with cold as a stimulating device, fomentations ease disorders of a sluggish liver or hurtful gall bladder. A smooth piece of ice rubbed over the affected area will also cause dispersion of circulating wastes; or, wrap a washcloth in a piece of ice and rub gently over aching area.

7. As part of a winter cold therapy, fomentations may well turn the tide and hasten the recovery rate.

8. Fomentations vigorously promote elimination of toxic substances by the sweating process and this is the greatest benefit. They are partners with controlled fasting in expelling toxic wastes.

FOOT BATH BENEFITS

When heat is applied to the body, blood vessels expand and the nerves experience a relaxation; for greater effectiveness, combine fomentations with a foot bath since this sends a feeling of warmth throughout the entire body and increases the effectiveness of local heat application. This foot-bath and fomentation combination stimulates the blood vessels lying under the skin and helps move impacted debris so the region can enjoy an internal washing by a flow of fresh blood. There is a reflex action with nerves in the feet which should be taken advantage of.

After the final treatments, the person should remain indoors until completely dry and until the body temperature is normal again. If possible, the person should remain in bed throughout the cooling-off session to ensure the most favorable response.

CONTRAST BATHS

You may have heard of contrast baths; indeed, they were utilized back in the days of Babylon; in fact, ancient kings and royalists overcame ailments by utilization of contrast baths that were described in that ancient of ancient collection of tales, *Thousand and One Nights*. Throughout the centuries, the contrast bath has served to ease pain, restimulate sluggish circulation, improve blood flow and help to cleanse and flush out internal wastes. They are tremendously effective in conjunction with controlled fasting.

Alternate hot-and-cold applications speed up the blood flow to the region being treated and this increase in nutrition and removal of cell wastes and tissue residues helps hasten body recovery, especially with the help of controlled fasting.

A director of the Hydrotherapy Department at a leading sanitarium, tells us this:

> For a bruised or injured hand or finger, an injury or infection of the foot, no better simple remedy has been found. The antibiotics and other advances of modern medicine make their contribution, but in addition to these measures, your physician will often recommend the contrast bath.
>
> It is important that an area larger than that injured be immersed in the bath. For instance, if you have an infected finger, choose a container large enough to cover the entire forearm up to the elbow. If the foot or leg is involved, a bath up to the knee, and in some cases well up on the thigh, is recommended. By using a large container, you will affect the blood vessels of a large area.
>
> *The push-and-pull action on the blood vessels that occurs as a result of using first hot and then cold, is the principle on which the treatment is based, for it brings a fresh blood supply to the area and aids the blood in carrying away waste products produced by the inflammation or injury. Nature is aided in the process of restoration.*
>
> For deep and effective healings, controlled fasting can trigger the most complete expulsion of body poisons.

WHAT YOU WILL NEED. To make a contrast bath, you will need the following: (1) Two containers large enough so the water can come well up over the treated part. (2) A bath thermometer so water temperature can be determined. A decided difference in temperature helps produce more favorable results. (3) A goodly supply of ice. (4) A clean, dry bath towel.

HOW TO TAKE A CONTRAST BATH

Put the affected arm or leg in hot water (105°F.) for three to four minutes; remove and put in cold water (tap or ice water) from 30 to 60 seconds (note the short cold water treatment). Unless otherwise otherwise indicated, *always* begin with hot water and end with cold. Continue this contrast method for six times. Dry thoroughly. That's all there is to it! You may repeat this six-time contrast bath throughout the day at different intervals.

PRECAUTIONS

Temperatures above 105°F. are not to be used for arm and leg blood vessel diseases nor for diabetes. Massage may also be contraindicated so your doctor's advice must always be sought. And again — you start with the hot and end with the cold. Use the thermometer to test water temperature. Put ice in the container of cold water to keep it good and cold.

APPLICATIONS FOR VARIOUS AILMENTS

INFECTION

For infectious ailments, the contrast between hot and cold should be as great as you can endure it. Begin with 110°F. and continue adding hot water to increase to tolerance. For cold application, start with ice water — keep adding more ice to maintain this cold temperature. And . . . end with the ice water treatment.

ANKLE SPRAIN

After the contrast bath, apply an ice bag or ice compress to the sprained ankle or other limb. Follow same instructions as for infection.

ARTHRITIS (Osteoarthritis)

Begin with 110°F. water and soak for 4 minutes. Change to container of tap water and immerse for 1 minute. Continue for 6 contrasts. There is an exception here — end with hot water. Add hot water so temperature is gradually increased to 115° F. - 120° F. After several sessions, tap water should have added ice so it is colder. Do this contrast bath remedy twice a day.

WEAK, PAINFUL FEET

Follow instructions for arthritis.

BLOOD VESSEL AILMENT

Traced to poor circulation. Soak limb in hot water (105°F.) for 3 minutes. Change to cold or ice water for 30 seconds. Contrast for 6 times and end with cold immersion.

ACHING EYES

Use small gauze squares or two small washcloths. Prepare two containers, one with hot water, the other with cold. Dip cloths in these alternate waters, wring nearly dry, apply over the eyes. *Note carefully:* your eyes are sensitive to heat so the hot cloth should be comfortable and not burn. After a few seconds, the cloth cools so apply the cold water cloth. Do this for 10 minutes. Heat and cold can be applied to other facial areas that need stimulation. I wonder if our ageless Hollywood queens use this fomentation method as their beauty secret?

VARICOSE VEINS

Follow same method as for infection — *but* — one exception: the cold application should *equal* that of the hot. For example, if you immerse a leg in hot water for 60 seconds, it should be immersed in the cold water for the same 60 seconds. About 60 seconds in the cold is about all most folks can take. So your home remedy may last from 15 to 20 minutes. Those troubled with unsightly leg veins should know that internal toxins have accumulated and caused infection and should respond to this internal washing method.

HEADACHES

Follow same instructions as for aching eyes. Apply contrast cloths to forehead and *especially* to the back of your neck. Muscle contractions caused by tension are often responsible for headaches. The muscle contractions cause an irritation of nerves in the cervical (neck) area; often, even a slight displacement of one of the vertebrae. The displacement or irritation then interrupts a normal flow of nerve energy to various body parts, interfering with the ability of the organs to properly function. The contrast applications to the back of the neck help stimulate sluggish blood flow and wash away the accumulation of dead cells and tissue wastes that become harmfully irritating and cause headaches.

SINUS PROBLEMS

An application of radiant heat will help relieve the congestion about the sinus openings; the sinuses are hollow resonance chambers in the front part of the skull below, above and behind the ears. Apply radiant heat or infrared when sitting because this position permits better drainage. Use a goose-neck lamp with a reflecting surface behind it. Either a large electric light bulb or regular infrared bulb sold at most drugstores is suitable. Place the lamp about 20 inches away from the face; if the heat is too much, move it further back. Cover eyes with two pieces of moist gauze or cotton that is held in place by a string around the head. Expose the entire face to this heat for about 15 minutes. After the treatment, bathe face in cool water. The heat causes an increased flow of fresh blood to the face and helps slough off accumulated toxic wastes that have caused the congestion. Do not go out in the cold weather after this remedy; remain indoors for one hour. If this heat application causes perspiration, cool off with a bath or an alcohol rub to prevent chilling.

OVER-ALL IMPROVEMENT

Remember the hot foot bath for relief of nervous tension, body aches, tiredness, headache, colds, coughs. When you warm your feet, you cause these blood vessels to dilate, easing congestion in your brain, lungs and abdominal organs. This circulation balance relieves congestion that is centered in any body part. A hot foot bath should be enjoyed every other night from ten to thirty minutes. Soak feet in a tub or large basin. The room should be draft-free. Start with temperature of 104°F. and gradually increase to 115°F. The head should be kept cool with a cold compress. After a dunking, remove feet, douse quickly with cold water (include soles and tops), dry the feet well. Rub with alcohol and have a good night's sleep!

HOW TO TURN INTO A "SPONGE"

Yes, you can turn yourself into a sponge by means of fomentations and contrast baths. These ancient remedies help bring a good blood supply to the congested area, cause profuse perspiration and this flow washes out the toxic wastes from your insides. Your skin is rich with blood vessels and nerves which are, in turn, connected to blood vessels and nerves of the internal organs. Fomentations and contrast baths cause local dilation of the blood vessels which lead to your internal organs and like a gigantic internal river, help wash away the wastes. You might say these health techniques "mop up" the outward flow of toxic poisons caused by controlled fasting.

This ancient home remedy stimulates circulation of your entire body. This is not a small matter because one-thirteenth of body weight is blood and about one third is lymph, that straw-colored fluid in the blood that must be kept free and clean of toxic wastes. Fomentations draw extra blood to the area, improve metabolism and wash out your insides and leave you sparkling clean . . . like a sponge!

Internal Washing Benefits as Outlined in This Chapter

1. Fomentations, moist heat applications, relax painful muscles and joint aches as well as a variety of other body pains.
2. Try fomentations for such ailments as chest colds, nervous disorders, neuralgic pains, arthritic problems, inflammation, etc.
3. Contrast baths help clean out toxic waste accumulations.
4. Follow suggestions for such ailments as infection, ankle sprains, arthritis, weak, painful feet, blood vessel disorder, aching eyes, varicose veins, headaches, sinus problems.
5. Foot baths give over-all improvement by stimulating sluggish circulation and helping to wash away toxic waste accumulations.
6. Controlled fasting makes the above health techniques all the more effective by cleansing the body internally for a complete "mop-up."

19

Guidelines for Starting and Ending Fasts

This chapter is a practical blueprint, for those guidelines that tell you how to start and progress and end your controlled fasting plan. Your faithful adherence to these guidelines will regulate your health progress with controlled fasting.

BEFORE YOU BEGIN

Plan for the controlled fasting regime. Set aside the one day or one week or even the one-month schedule. Plan for it in advance and prepare yourself mentally for the program. Gradually, decrease your consumption of devitalized foods, decrease your intake of sugars and starches. Substitute with more and more natural foods and, particularly, more and more fresh fruits and vegetables. This readies your system for the program.

WHERE TO FAST

Preferably, fast at home, if you can, but if you go to work, then fast while eating out. That's right — you eat while you fast, but you substitute unnatural foods with natural foods. If you can, bring your own lunch with you. Your atmosphere should be one of contentment and free from temptations. Pure air and pure water should also be available. If you can take a vacation in a healthy, country environment, so much the better. If not, every night try to get into a fresh air section of your vicinity. Surely there must be some little park, some little countryside where you can breathe in some fresh air. This is important as it helps cleanse out your insides. Foods eaten should be fresh and pure — throughout this book, I have given you special diets and controlled fasting programs for a score of different ailments that may be traced to conditions of internal toxemia. If you want such programs to succeed, you must breathe in pure air, drink pure water and eat the foods described — but these should be organically grown and raised. Ask at a local health food store for a source of supply.

SAVE ENERGY

Avoid unnecessary expenditure of energy. Conserve your strength during the controlled fasting program. Avoid situations that contribute to tension or nervous disorders.

GET YOUR REST

Forget partying at least temporarily, or special types of entertainment which means you'll be surrounded by spicy foods, noise and after-midnight merrymaking. You need your good night's rest. Get a healthy night's sleep, and go to sleep "refreshed."

PROPER VENTILATION

When indoors, see that your room is well ventilated, day or night.

WARMTH

Chilling causes discomfort and prevents rest and sleep and checks elimination of body wastes. Warmth promotes comfort and good elimination of body wastes. A comfortable body temperature is important so keep yourself warm so that your reserves of vitality may be conserved. Nerve force and nerve energy is required to keep you warm; if you're chilled, it means a rapid dissipation of this vital nerve force so keep warm and save your nerves.

EXERCISE

See Chapter 20 for rules about exercise. Keep your body active while fasting. That is, don't just sit in a chair. Go about your activities but with a minimum of strain. *Avoid fatigue!*

BATHING

Take a comfortable tub bath to wash away the substances excreted by your body. A too-hot or too-cold bath may deplete energy so stay in your tub for about 5 minutes. Water should be comfortable.

SUNBATHING

The sun is healthy but don't overdo it. Avoid heat of the day as this may exhaust you. Enervation may be caused by excess. When I fast, I usually sunbathe for five minutes exposure to my front surface, then five minutes to my back surface. Gradually, I increase one minute each day until my exposure time is 15 minutes. That's my limit. You may find it satisfactory for yourself, too.

BAD MOUTH TASTE

As your body gives off wastes during a fast, you'll feel this bad mouth taste. Alleviate it with a tongue scrubbing. That's right — use a clean natural bristle tooth brush and scrub your tongue. Mouth washes and gargles depend upon your own individual preferences. Rinse with ordinary warm water, regularly, for a clean mouth effect. Peculiarly enough, bad mouth taste is an indication body poisons are being expelled.

WATER DRINKING

Flush out wastes with tap water. Avoid ice water since this constricts various body muscles and may hinder circulation.

BE OF GOOD CHEER

When you're hungry, you may be grouchy! But when you're on a controlled fasting plan, you're not hungry because you continue to eat — and your fare is natural so you're spared the ravages of chemical residue in some commonly accepted foods, and this should make you feel cheerful. If possible, avoid gloomy situations. This is a good time to read humorous books, see humorous theatricals and — often — have a good and healthy laugh!

HOW TO END CONTROLLED FASTING

Frankly, once you discover which foods build your health and which foods destroy it, you should continue on this dietary-improvement program. But if you feel reasonably relieved from your ailments, you may go back to your previous eating habits — but you must *eliminate permanently* those foods which have caused your ailments. Otherwise, you just defeat yourself. End your controlled fasting program by letting yourself indulge in a little "luxury" of an occasional pastry or devitalized concoction. I think that you, like thousands of others who have been put back on the road to health by controlled fasting, will have an aversion for these sugary-sweet and artificially spiced foods. Controlled fasting has a miraculous, almost magical way of erasing your desire for such artificial edibles that work on undermining your health.

WHEN TO END CONTROLLED FASTING

As stated above, you do not get yourself cured only to revert back to habits that caused your illness. But if you rigidly follow a special program that will end in favor of introducing more natural foods, then you may end when the following recoveries are noted: you have a natural appetite. Your breath becomes clean and sweet. Your tongue becomes clean, after it has had a thick coating due to the fact of being clogged with toxicity. Your body temperature which may have been under-or over-normal is now normal. Your pulse has a normal rhythm. Your skin glows. You have no bad mouth taste. Your salivary secretion is normalized. You have better sight, better hearing, better energy and an optimistic viewpoint on life. Furthermore, when your urine is light, it means your insides have been washed clean. You never felt so well and good! That's as simple as I can put it for you.

ONE-DAY FAST PLAN

Breakfast consists of raw juices. For something to chew on, a mixture of wheat germ with mashed bananas. Lunch consists of raw vegetable juices. For something to chew on, lettuce, celery and raw cabbage. Dinner consists of raw vegetable juices again in any desired combination. For the chewing instinct, a baked potato with butter pat and raw carrot strips. Throughout the day, drink a glass of freshly squeezed raw juice, or fruit or vegetable to ease the urge to eat.

SPEEDY ONE WEEK FAST-AND-EAT INTERNAL CLEANSING PLAN

On all *odd*-numbered days of the week, you devote yourself to fruit. Drink freshly squeezed fruit juices in desired combinations . . . and for eating, take the pulp and eat with a spoon! Delicious and filling! On all *even*-numbered days of the week, you devote yourself to vegetables. Again, drink freshly squeezed vegetable or fruit juices in desired mixtures . . . and then eat the pulp! You will automatically receive an abundance of precious vitamins, minerals, proteins and those body-sustaining, life-giving enzymes!

NATURE'S GOLDEN DOZEN TONICS
FOR APPETITE TAMING

Here are favorite health tonics that help ease appetite, reduce that hunger compulsion, soothe stomach pangs and help melt unwanted pounds like ice in a furnace because they are low-low-low calorie and of high-high-high nutrient value. These tonics, prepared from natural fruits and vegetables will help perform a unique "inside cleansing" action that sweep out debris from your "innards."

1. Mix together, chill and then serve this beverage: 1 cup coconut juice, 1 cup papaya juice, ½ cup pineapple juice, ½ cup fresh orange juice.

2. Mix well, together, chill and drink this beverage: 1 cup red cherry juice, 1 cup strawberry juice, ½ cup pineapple juice, ¼ cup lemon juice.

3. Combine these juices, chill and serve: 2 quarts white grape juice, the juice of four oranges, the juice of one lemon, ½ cup pineapple juice, ½ cup cherry juice.

4. Clean and scrape 6 large juicy carrots. Clean 4 large celery stalks. Put through juicer. Add ¼ cup coconut milk. Stir well and drink.

5. Liquefy 4 sprigs watercress in 1 cup tomato juice. Add 1 cup celery juice. Mix together and drink.

6. *Flaxeed Tea.* Wash 1/4 cup flaxeed thoroughly, drain, add boiling water. Boil gently for 2 hours. Drain. Season with 2 tablespoons lemon juice. When cool, sip slowly.

7. Liquefy and serve these foods: 2 glasses pineapple juice, 4 young tender dandelion leaves, 4 tender lettuce leaves, 2 sprigs parsley and 4 pitted dates.

8. *Cambric Tea.* Add 1/4 glass milk to 3/4 glass boiling water; sweeten with honey according to taste. Sip slowly.

9. *Vegetable Broth.* Combine carrots, parsley, celery, tomato, string beans, green peas, squash in enough water to cover. Bring to a boil, turn flame low and let simmer until vegetables are done. Strain and serve. This is a meal in itself !

10. Add 1 teaspoon of sour cream to each glass of milk. Mix well, pour in separate glasses and place in a warm spot for 30 hours. (Yes, this has to be prepared in advance.) Mix once only during this time. Do not cover glasses tightly. When milk has thickened, put in refrigerator and keep there until serving time. This, too, can be a meal in itself, especially for lunch.

11. Place one cup of dry soya beans in a pan and put in a 350°F. oven for about 90 minutes. Turn occasionally while roasting. When cool, grind, but not too fine, about the same as coffee is ground. Try a blender for a grinder. Put one heaping spoonful in a pint of boiled water. Let it boil for 4 minutes, lower heat for 15 minutes, then serve. Add honey to taste. This is a wonderful coffee substitute, chock full of protein and minerals, not to mention vitamins.

12. A glass of simple cucumber juice — one of the richest sources of phosphorus, sodium, calcium, sulphur, silicon. Also rich in vitamins. A wonderful thirst and hunger quencher.

IMPORTANCE OF JUICER AND BLENDER EQUIPMENT

You should purchase a juicer and a blender as your fasting equipment. Ask at any health store or housewares department for different models that are priced at various levels. I do urge you to get these machines as you will then be able to prepare your juices right at home and also be able *to eat the pulp left over.* Now, you may not be able to prepare your own coconut juice or other juices, so ask your health store for a can of it. Most stores have these juices in canned form.

A MAN'S GUIDE TO FASTING SUCCESS

When controlled fasting is combined with a general over-all health improvement program, it stands a better chance for success. Here are easy-to-follow health suggestions to be utilized together with your fasting schedule. This guide is for men. The women readers will find their guide at the end of this one. Now, hear this, you men:

1. Begin your day with a brisk walk, if only for five minutes. As you walk, take deep breaths. This gives you a renewed stamina that puts power in your mind and your body.

2. Eat lunch away from your office or place of business. Walk to that place. Find a quiet place where you can eat in slow relaxation. Do not talk business while eating. This helps digestion. If you must lunch with a business associate, suggest that you first eat and then you talk. This helps you think better, too.

3. Periodically, take a few minutes of relaxation. If you can, lie down on a reclining chair or couch. Many office men have these for their relaxation use. Or, let your arms slump, your head sink. Erase and blot out everything from your mind. If you do this every three hours, you'll be astonished at how your strength and energy will be revitalized. Take this 10-minute internal-charging rest break and you'll help rebuild your health as the days go on.

4. For a pick-up, remember a glass of fresh fruit or vegetable juice. Rich in nutrients, you'll feel more energetic after one glass. If you want to chew on something, stay away from starches and cookies and eat some fruit. Keep fresh fruit in your drawer or by your work site, in a paper bag. Bring the fruit with you from home.

You'll be surprised at the lift this will give you.

5. If you're tired, stand up, *stretch, stretch, stretch!* On your toes, reach for the ceiling. This takes the kinks out of your shoulders and spine, clears the fog from your mind, revitalizes your thought process. Do this regularly.

6. A vacation is Nature's prescription. Take a vacation in the country, away from the noise and stench of the city. Try a weekend vacation periodically too. You'll be amazed at how you will be rejuvenated by a change of scenery.

7. Find an interest in some physically stimulating activity — boating, tennis playing, swimming, even hiking. Get your doctor's okay, first. Remember fishing? So few of us seem to remember this wonderfully relaxing entertainment. Try gardening, too. Anything to give you an opportunity to commune with Nature.

8. Be sociable. Have a lot of friends. No man is an island unto himself. Mix with others to ease tensions. Good companionship is important — but don't let it interfere with your peace of mind and nightly rest.

9. "Sorry, but I'm on special orders not to eat or drink that! I'll have some fruit juice, instead, if you don't mind." That's all you have to say when your host or hostess offers you a food or beverage taboo on your controlled fasting list. If you are in a bind and have to join others in a special toast, take the undesirable beverage, toast with the others by raising the glass, put it to your lips but don't drink! As for smokes, if you must take cigars, put it in your pocket "for tomorrow."

10. And, remember your controlled fasting plan, the foods you should eat and those which you should not.

Difficult? Not really, unless you make it so!

A WOMAN'S GUIDE TO FASTING SUCCESS

Housewives and career gals can succeed with controlled fasting if they utilize these tips for over-all health and good looks:

1. Plan ahead. Know exactly what you're going to do either on your job or at home (or both) and be rigid about your schedule. Give yourself as much work as you can healthfully and happily handle. No more. Otherwise, you'll injure yourself and your family.

2. Follow a generally organized life plan. Rule out those situations, circumstances and occurrences that displease you or create

disharmony. Cancel them out of your life. Blot them from your mind. Use thoughts for constructive purposes only.

3. Daily, you *must* have a rest period. This is not a luxury. This is a treasured necessity. Women, today, carry great burdens as their responsibilities increase and they must have good health to meet the challenge of business and/or home. Take a daily rest period of 10 to 20 minutes. This will indeed be the pause that will refresh and rejuvenate you. Compromise with life. First things come first — and your health is at the top of that list!!

4. Keep regular hours. Sleep is essential so don't sacrifice sleep for any purpose except some extra-special emergency. Let the others burn the midnight oil and burn themselves out. A good night's sleep is a wonderful tonic that you can't beg, borrow or steal.

5. For a revitalizing pick-up, a glass of fresh fruit juice or any fresh fruit is a good idea.

6. Daily, relax for just ten minutes by stretching out on a couch or bed. Close your eyes. All your limbs become very limp, like a rag doll — and your mind should be just as blank and non-existent as a rag doll.

7. Daily, take a warm bath; afterward, rub yourself with a body lotion, put on comfortable clothes and go about your household duties. You working gals can do this when you come home. It's refreshing.

8. Food should be natural. Omit cakes, cookies, ice cream, cola drinks, sodas, pastries, etc. This starch foods create internal toxemia that will ultimately lead to impaired health.

9. Your meals should contain wholesome foods. For your family, give them much fresh fruits and vegetables. Eliminate foods that contain chemicals, preservatives or have been processed as these are unnatural.

10. Smile. Be happy. Look on the bright side of things. I once knew an 88-year-old great-great-grandmother who told me her secret for happiness. Said this fine woman, "My mind and thoughts are like a sun dial — they record only what is bright and cheerful." Radiate cheer and happiness — others will be attracted to you.

Chapter Highlights in a Nutshell

1. Plan ahead for your fasting program. Select a place to fast. Save energy. Breathe fresh air, keep warm, be of good cheer.

2. End fasting when you feel in tip-top shape and "glad all over."
3. For a sample, try a one day fast plan; or, a one week fast-and-eat plan. Above all, remember to eat what is natural if you want your rejuvenated health to remain with you.
4. Try some of the Golden Dozen health tonics. Some can be substituted for a meal.
5. Build the 10-point guide to fasting success into your life for better health and happiness.

20

How to "Exer-Fast" for Extra Health Benefits

There is life in movement. There is rust in immobility. If you could take a good look at your insides, you would discover the ravages of *internal pollution*. Clinging to your arteries would be clumps of crust and refuse; cluttering up your bloodstream would be an accumulation of debris. The delicate digestive, respiratory, circulatory organs would be tinged with refuse. Compare this situation to a landlocked lake or pool of water, choked in by barriers, infested with debris, wastes, pollutants, refuse and sewage. When this cesspool is given an outlet, permitted to move and to circulate, the wastes are gradually eliminated and gradually the water is sparkling fresh and clean. Yes, there *is* life in movement and that applies to your body.

Movement is more than walking to your auto or railroad station, a few steps from your home. Movement is more than going from one office desk to the next. Movement is more than going from the refrigerator to the dining table. Movement is a planned program of physical fitness and exercise designed to stimulate your insides, to revitalize the sluggish internal systems and help refresh them. As part of your controlled fasting plan to obtain health, exercise is a vital feature. The "Exer-Fast" method is a combination of simply performed exercises during the controlled fasting period. Together, exercise and controlled fasting becomes a double-barrel effect in cleaning out your insides.

When You Are Well. Your body is a complicated machine and every part interacts upon other parts. During exercise, not only do you lubricate your muscles, but you also improve the functioning of other organs. Exercise maintains body tone.

What Is Body Tone? This is a term used to describe the condition of the body. Good tone is the opposite of flabby or limp. When you have good body tone, your muscles, skin, organs, blood vessels and all its other parts are in good condition, healthy, properly hydrated, getting rid of waste materials properly and operating at optimum level without fatigue or loss of quality. Your body needs to operate actively or it will lose this body tone. When the body is allowed to "rust," waste materials accumulate and lead to internal stagnation like a dirt and pollution-infested pond.

What Exercise Does for You. Exercise developes muscles in the male, shapeliness in the female. The body has over 600 muscles which make possible every movement. The muscles do such things as pass food along the digestive tract, maintain posture, suck air into the lungs and tighten blood vessels to elevate the blood pressure when more pressure is needed in an emergency. Your heart, too, is a muscular pump.

Exercise and Circulation. Exercise stimulates fresh and clean circulation. When all body muscles are exercised, circulation speeds up to furnish more oxygen to these muscles and remove waste material. The faster your cells receive oxygen, the better you feel. You "come alive." This increased activity sends more fresh and clean blood to your brain and makes you more alert.

Helps Internal Organs. The faster action of the circulatory system helps the functioning of your internal organs. Your heart becomes stronger and steadier; your lungs are capable of taking in more oxygen; elimination of body wastes is properly performed. Without exercise, toxic wastes remain within and this leads to weariness and fatigue.

Builds Endurance. A fit person can work better than one who is weak or out of condition; he can do the job with the same amount of effort and with less energy; he can perform more tasks with less tiring effect. This explains why many men in the 40's and 50's are being pushed out in favor of younger ones, in business, in factories, in industry. The older men are too tired. But they were once more vigorous and energetic. What happened? They let themselves get lazy, shiftless, victims of "sititis" and spectators rather than activists. "Exer-Fast" can counteract the ravages of internal pollution.

Helps Strengthen Mind and Body. Being physically fit also helps to improve mind and body. Exercise cleans out the mind and refreshes the body. As for youngsters, if they can get in a good exercise program, they feel and sleep better. After sitting in the classroom for seven to eight hours, it is not good for them to settle for too long in front of the television set. Stagnation hits the youngsters, too!

HOW EXERCISE HELPS CLEAN YOUR INSIDES DURING FASTING

"It will come as a shock to the sedentary male," says Professor Thomas Kirk Cureton of the University of Illinois, "to learn that his body was middle-aged by the time he was 26." The Professor found that the average person in the 40's is so sedentary that he cannot climb a flight of stairs without getting somewhat out of breath. "He is only one emotional shock or one sudden exertion away from a serious heart attack."

Professor Cureton who is in charge of the University's famous Physical Fitness Research Laboratory has found that internal pollution caused by lack of exercise can lead to many illnesses. He points to these cleansing benefits, which are accelerated with controlled fasting.

1. Regular exercise frees the clumps of cholesterol so that you can eat without fear of an abnormal raising of blood cholesterol level.
2. Exercise prevents the weakening of the abdominal wall which leads to the unsightly "pot belly" — in men and women!
3. Regular exercise develops additional blood channels (collateral circulation) allowing more flow wherever blood is needed, including the heart.
4. Lung congestion because of lymph accumulation may be reduced or prevented by full use of the lungs in exercise.
5. There is evidence that the toxic wastes of cholesterol and serum triglycerides, both fatty wastes which clog arteries and contribute to cardiovascular ailment, can be sloughed off by regular exercise.
6. Regular exercise builds up the health of the heart's network of tiny

vessels supplying oxygen, cleansing these vessels, washing them and thereby providing a valuable safeguard against heart trouble.

7. Exercise redistributes weight, helps melt excess fat, cleanses your insides so you can meet the challenges of heat, cold, stress, anxiety, tension, much more easily.

REGULAR CONTINUOUS PROGRAM IS ESSENTIAL

Often I hear men say, "Every Saturday and Sunday I swim 10 laps in our club pool. Brother, am I getting in shape." What they fail to realize is that any so-called workout which fails to stress the heart and circulatory system for at least 30 minutes also fails to "wash" the circulatory system. Short, violent workouts or those too-casual exercise sessions done over a very long period do not touch the glycogen stores in the liver; muscle proteins remain practically intact and the fat deposits are not called upon for their excess stores.

Continuous, rhythmical exercise, in particular a combination of exercise with fasting that takes place for at least 30 minutes will stir up the stagnant pools of waste materials and start to cleanse out the insides. This means that you should devote at least three "Exer-Fast" sessions per week, for at least 30 minutes each session.

"Exer-Fast" combinations will cause a dilation of the blood vessels and concommitant increase in the volume of fresh and clean blood rushing to wash out the heart-lung circuit as well as the entire cardiovascular system.

"Exer-Fast" aids the circulatory system to be cleansed while the heart-lung circuit is super-charged with fresh and vital oxygen and nutrient supply. The network of blood vessels remains in a dilated state while the blood is recapturing its needed supply of fresh and toxemia-free oxygen. "Exer-Fast" produces a speedier lowering of blood fat (cholesterol) and blood pressure due to peripheral resistance or other forms of hypertension. "Exer-Fast" helps to reopen the capillaries, forcing open the microscopic blood vessels which carry nutrients to the tissues.

Lack of proper exercise, even if you follow the principles of controlled fasting, will still cause the capillaries to recede, for as the circulatory system loses its elasticity and as the flow of blood decreases due to ptosis (drooping or sagging of some body part such as the eyelid or abdomen), it fails to reach the tissues as it did when you were more physically active.

"Exer-Fast" helps reopen the capillaries by maintaining blood flow under higher pressures and under stress for longer time periods; this method develops collateral circulation wherein additional blood vessels other than the major vessels are established. When this collateral circulation is established by means of "Exer-Fast" it means that you have a better survival rate in the event of a coronary occlusion or other heart ailment.

STRETCH ... STRETCH ... STRETCH ...

Throughout the day, if you will stretch yourself, it is a helpful way of stimulating the stagnant pools within you. This is the simplest type of exercise to be used in conjunction with your controlled fasting. Dr. Cureton suggests you do full range movements to the full capacity of your joints and chest cage. He adds, "When connective tissue is not actively elongated (by means of stretching), it steadily shortens. If it carries a constant load it thickens and this may cause an irritating pressure on nerves passing through it. Such irritations can feed back to upset the delicate balance of the autonomic nervous system and the endocrine system.

"Stretching usually relieves neck and lower back pains and relieves neuromuscular hypertension anywhere. *Stretching in directions opposite to gravitational force is generally implied.*"

Try this exercise right now: slowly bend your head backward on your shoulders but do not move the rest of your body. Move it back ... back ... back ... down ... down ... down until you think it is between your shoulder blades and everything looks topsy turvy. Count to 10. Slowly, bring your head upright again. Did you feel the alternate contractions and expansions? Everything swerves, then steadies. Count to 10. Repeat. Do this for five sessions at the same half hour. Alternate by lifting your arms all the way and try to touch the ceiling. Repeat five times. Breathe in as you raise up on your tiptoes. Count to 10. Breathe out as you slowly go down on your feet and lower your arms. This is a simple exercise yet highly effective as it starts to move the stagnation pools in the back of your neck and your shoulders.

During your program of controlled fasting, you should devote at least 30 to 45 minutes every night to any of these exercises in any combination. Vary these exercises so you don't get too much of the same ones. After all, you want over-all body improvement rather than just one part. Here are the exercises to be utilized during your controlled fasting plan.

SPECIAL "EXER-FAST" EXERCISES

1. Assume a diver's stance. Arms outstretched. Stand on tiptoes with eyes closed. Keep this stance and your balance for the count of 30.
2. Squat with your palms on the floor. Tip forward; rest your legs on your elbows. Toes are off the floor in a squat handstand. Count to 15.
3. A forefinger touches the floor. Walk in a circle around it for 8 times in a 30 second session. Then walk a straight 5-foot line within 10 seconds.
4. Both knees are straight, legs are together. Bend at your waist and touch the ground with your fingertips. You women should touch the ground with your palms.
5. Sit down. Slowly bend from this same seated position — keep knees flat — until your forehead is a two fist length away from the ground. Count to 10. Repeat 5 times.
6. Flat on your tummy. Feet are pinned to the ground. Lace fingers behind your neck nape, lift up chin until it is about 15 inches from the ground.
7. Kneel with insteps flat on the ground. Move just arms and back as you spring erect, both feet together. Keep this balance for count of 5. Repeat 10 times.
8. Stand erect. Touch your toes at waist height but do NOT bend your legs. Repeat 10 times speedily.
9. Here is a 6-part exercise. Squat. Kick your legs backwards. Kick them forward between your arms. Turn over. Squat. Hop to your feet.
10. This is for you rugged men, although health-conscious women may want to try it, too. A partner is needed. The partner is lying down and should be close to your own weight. Lift and carry your partner — fireman style — in a 10-second pickup from floor to

pickup. The partner lies horizontally across your shoulders with head on one side and legs on the other while you hold him. Do it just once.

11. Put both hands on your hips as you lie down. Your partner bends on one knee, reaches under your shoulders, lifts you up — but you must keep your body rigid for 45 seconds. This is a good way to strengthen coordination.

12. Lie flat. Stretch out your arms, palms flat on ground. Lift up *only* your midsection about 5 inches in an extended press-up. The rest of your body is rigid. Women may use forearms to balance upon instead of palms. Good to tighten tummy muscles and prevent pot belly by sending accumulated wastes streaming out of your midsection.

13. Do a standing broad jump to your height length. If you're under 30, the distance is the same as your height plus 12 inches.

14. Do 10 complete push-ups with your palms flat on the ground but positioned beneath your shoulders. Keep those knees straight!

15. Chin yourself about 20 times. If you have no chin bar, lie down flat on your back, lock fingers together, get a partner to lift you by your hands and pull you up until your chest strikes his knees. Keep the rest of your body rigid.

16. Sit on the ground. Keep knees stiff. Put hands on hips. Lean back, let your legs lift from the floor in a V-sit and hold 45 seconds.

17. Run in the same place for 120 seconds at double-time. Then stop. Take five deep breaths — hold each breath for 30 seconds.

18. Do a set of two-foot hops, straddle hops, scissor or alternate stride, hops.

"EXER-FAST" PROGRAM FOR BUSY BUSINESSMEN

Deskbound means stagnation. Here are some suggestions for simple exercises during your controlled fasting program which, I assume, is taking place as you keep on working:

1. Never sit longer than one hour without getting up and moving about the office.

2. When your phone rings, stand up to answer. As you listen, suck in your tummy hard, hold it until you have to breathe again or have to talk.

3. When you receive a visitor, stand up beside your chair, contract the thigh muscles hard and hold as tight as possible for 60

seconds or longer.

4. When you dismiss a visitor, get up but DO NOT USE THE CHAIR ARMS FOR SUPPORT. Let your body muscles push you up — and when you sit down, do not touch the chair arms.

IN-THE-OFFICE EXERCISES

These may be easily carried out when you are alone in your office:

1. Seize your chair arms and lift your body from the chair for six times. Gradually work up to 30 up and down motions.
2. Sit back in your chair. Straighten both legs before you. Lift them (keep those knees stiff) straight up as high as possible. Hold for count of 25.
3. Stand up. Roll your head in a circle. Right to left, then left to right. (This is a wonderful exercise for those who must bend over a desk or typewriter most of the day. Feel those kinks snapping? I did this same exercise daily for a 15 session period while I wrote this book and it really cleansed my thinking capacities. Otherwise, I become stiff and foggy while hunched over my typewriter.)
4. Pull up your shoulders, to your ears. Roll them forward with all your strength. Quickly, thrust back and hold for the count of 15. Rest. Repeat 15 times.
5. Lean forward against your desk. Move legs until they are back as far as possible. With arms only, push your body away from desk until it is supported by hands and arms. This is an "office push-up" to be performed 10 times.
6. Hop in position. Drop into a half-knee bend, jump forward, let your feet leave the floor by about four inches. Repeat 10 times.

SAUNA BATH

Your "Exer-Fast" program will have a stronger success rate if you can avail yourself of a sauna bath. If you can join an athletic club with such facilities, it's wonderful. Perhaps you can afford to have one built in your house. Look in the classified section of your local telephone directory under Bath Houses and Gymnasiums and ask if any of these places have such a sauna bath. Ask at the physiotherapy department of a local hospital.

DRY HEAT HEALTH PRINCIPLE

The sauna bath works on a dry heat principle. Actually, it's quite simple. In Finland, a log hut is planned with a nest of rocks in the corner, under which the fire is built. When the rocks are heated red hot, a dry heat fills the room. During this bath, you slap your skin with birch leaves. The oil from the leaves penetrates the skin, acting as an irritant and making the skin rosy red. All the while, impurities are flushed out of the skin and the oil from the leaves enters the body as replacement.

After 15 to 30 minutes of a sauna, the bather jumps into a pool of ice water. Several hot-and-cold changes are followed with a rubdown. This sounds rugged. It is not to be embarked upon quickly. A gradual adjustment is necessary. But we do know that just about every Finn has such a sauna bath and few of them complain of clogged arteries or internal pollution; many Finns are nonagenarians. And we do know that you are as old as your arteries!!

The Sauna Bath Flushes Arteries. After an exercise session, a sauna bath is exceptionally beneficial. The quick change from hot steam to icy cold flushes out impurities and toxic wastes from the arterial structures. This method causes arterial dilation so the skin becomes rosy-red as toxic wastes are flushed out and fresh blood is brought to the surface. The icy water dip squeezes the arteries down tight, whisking the blood from the skin surface into the warmer viscera of the body.

This blood flushing stimulates circulation; it flushes any possible sludge from arteries, keeps the smooth-muscle walls of the arteries soft and elastic rather than allowing them to become encrusted with debris, wastes and claques to lead to arteriosclerosis. This method keeps your respiratory passages well moistened with steam, soothing them, helping to prevent coughs, too.

Skin blemishes are improved with the sauna and exercise principles. The increased blood circulation to the skin sparked by the hot steam causes free perspiration; pores are opened and out come the flushed oil, grit debris. You look healthy and youthful, free from toxemia.

BUILD EXERCISE INTO YOUR CONTROLLED FASTING PLAN

Set aside a special 30 to 60 minute nightly session for exercises while you rejuvenate your system with controlled fasting. At the same time, put power into your body machine by letting it walk more often. Walk as much as you can without tiring yourself. Walk to work. Walk to your shopping center. Walk to your neighbors. Wherever possible, walk.

Always sit in an erect position. Do not slump. When driving an auto, keep a small cushion in back of your shoulder blades while the small of your back rests against the back of your seat. In this position, the upper part of your spine is thrown forward; the small of your back, your head and shoulders — are all pushed slightly backwards — a position that helps to correct many spinal irregularities and pains of the sacroiliac and back.

Trouble with Backache? Lie on your back with your knees up; a cushion under your shoulder blades. Relax in this position for 15 minutes daily. You'll be amazed at how low back pains and generalized spinal troubles are eased with this simple exercise-position.

"Exer-Fast" should be built into your life, made part of your program to restore your body to the level of vigorous health that is your birthright. It's up to you! Nobody can do exercises for you! Good circulation is good health!

How "Exer-Fast" Can Revitalize a Tired Body

1. Combat problems of internal pollution by giving your body a lot of movement and exercises during your controlled fasting.
2. "Exer-Fast" restores body tones, strengthens digestive powers, washes out your insides, improves circulation, builds strength of mind and body.
3. Stretch . . . stretch . . . stretch to wash out your internal stagnant pools.
4. Select a set of any of the described easy-to-follow exercises and follow a regular nightly 30 or 60 minute exercise session.
5. If you can, take a sauna bath.
6. Businessmen and office workers should try the special exercises.
7. When driving, keep good posture.

21

How Fasting Will Soothe Your Nervous System

Nerves ... nerves ... nerves. Tension ... tension ... tension. Tired ... tired ... tired. Fatigue ... fatigue ... fatigue. Noise ... noise ... noise.

These are words that are products of our present day rush ... rush ... rush ... and we do live in nervous surroundings so we cannot blame ourselves completely for the physical and mental deterioration that results from chronic wear and tear on our nerves.

Any natural method that helps build resistance to tense surroundings is welcome in our modern times. If you are a nervous business man or woman, a housewife surrounded by stress situations, an average person who is a bundle of nerves, you may find a modicum of relief and even cure by means of controlled fasting. Improper foods can irritate the delicate nerves. D. G. Campbell, in *Modern Nutrition in Health and Disease,* tells us that the nervous system is more sensitive to nutritional variance than any other part of the body. He emphasizes the great importance of the B-complex vitamins for nerve food. Minerals are needed for nerve tissue.

WASTE-CREATING SUBSTANCES

The nerves react with trigger-sensitive spasms when subjected to chronic irritation by certain internal pollutants. Where do these toxic substances come from? Unnatural foods.

F. Avery Jones, M.D., in *The Practitioner,* tells us that nervous stress arises from excitement, anxiety, resentment, frustration, fatigue, insomnia, exposure and so forth and also from these ingested edibles:

1. Irregular meals.
2. Badly cooked foods, regardless of natural state.
3. Alcohol.
4. Irritation from chemical processing of foods.
5. Taking of laxatives.

Your first step is to correct the above conditions and go on a controlled fasting plan which *eliminates* chemically-drenched foods such as those refined foods, starches, sweets, sodas, processed cold cuts, frozen foods, cakes and pastries, etc. These introduce waste residue into the system and tend to irritate and torture the billions of delicate nerve endings in your system.

SPECIAL CONTROLLED FASTING PLAN

In a paper prepared by Norman Jolliffe, M.D., a respected authority on nutrition, the details were given of a special controlled fasting plan that strengthened nervous disorders by means of controlled fasting. Here is an outline of the plan used by the doctor:

1. A full, nutritious diet of natural, unrefined foods. No sugar, candy, jellies, white flour products, polished rice or alcohol drinks. Each day the patient gets citrus juices or tomato juice, milk, meat (including liver), eggs, butter, salad of raw vegetables and/or fruit, salad oil and potatoes. The balance of the diet is selected from vegetables, fruits and natural whole grain bread.
2. Vitamins by mouth include fish liver oil containing 10,000 units of Vitamin A, and a source of the entire B-complex (brewer's yeast, vegex, liver extract, wheat germ) — natural source.
3. Injections of the Vitamin B-complex in liver extract or as thiamin hydrochloride — 10 mg., riboflavin — 1 mg., and niacin — 100 mg.

The success rate was very favorable. Dr. Jolliffe healed his patients not only of nervous disorders but also of impending mental illness.

Each nerve is a thread of living tissue and these little fibers connect the brain cells with just about every body cell. Nerve cells resemble electric wires except that they are composed of soft tissue instead of metal. Each one consists of a central core surrounded by a membrane, thus resembling the wire in its insulating covering. Some of these nerves carry impulses from the brain to various organs and tissues, while others carry messages from these to the great central office in your head.

The membrane is delicate in that it reacts when "touched" by something artificial, harsh and irritating. That "something" is food — devitalized and unnatural food. So the very basis of controlled fasting for nerve strength is to eliminate unnatural foods from your diet.

9 WAYS TO MELT TENSION ALONG WITH FASTING

In the Good Book we read, "Man is born unto trouble, as the sparks fly upward." (Job 5:7.) We are born into conflict and tension so the method is learn how to face tension, how to react and how to cushion our nerves against excessive irritation. Here are 9 ways to melt tension:

1. *Do not have a bitter attitude.* My favorite philosopher, Lin Yutang, tells the story of the Oriental who stopped on his way home from work to purchase a pot of soya sauce. He fastened the pot to the end of a bamboo pole and began the journey home. Suddenly, the pot dropped off the pole and shattered. Someone saw it and yelled but the Oriental continued to walk without turning around. Finally, the passerby ran up to him, seized his arm and declared, "Don't you know your pot of soya sauce fell down and broke and spilled?" The Oriental retorted, "Yes, I heard it break. There's nothing I can do about it, so why should I let it detain me from getting home and enjoying the evening with my family?"

You would probably have reacted differently — like the fellow who stubbed his toe on a curb, became enraged, kicked the curb and shattered his foot. Being bitter only worsens everything.

2. *Do not surrender to your troubles.* Nervous people tend to embrace trouble. They become obsessed over it, obliterating any means of cure. Face your problem, analyze it, study it — and plan a means of solution. Conquer your troubles before they conquer you.

3. *Don't rationalize your blue mood by assuming that trouble will make you a better person.* A man rarely buttoned his collar. When asked for the reason, he explained, "I have a recurring rash on my neck and it irritates me to button my collar; but I suppose it's good to suffer a little and to learn patience." Whereupon someone asked, "If it's good to suffer, why don't you button your collar and increase the trouble?" This is good common sense. Look upon trouble as an enemy and try to conquer that enemy. The longer you

live and endure trouble, the greater will be your nervous problem.

4. *Learn to adjust.* Develop a flexible and bending attitude, like a sapling branch. The winds will blow against you, like a sapling, but will not break you if you learn to bend with the pressure. Adjust to the problem; be flexible as you try to solve the matter.

5. *Nervousness is here to stay.* Life is not all-perfect. You will face nervous situations, ups and downs, constant movement: Recognize this fact. The ocean is not always calm and quietly reflecting the sun. Often, the breakers heave and foam and roar tempestuously. Swim *with* the tide and not against it. Admit that there will be many nervous situations in your lifetime and learn to face them squarely.

6. *Cooperate with the opposition.* This sounds paradoxical and perhaps it is but it can work to ease tense situations. You can fight stubbornness by meeting it mid-way, offering some cooperation, then gradually winning the opposition over to your side. You cannot catch a fish by shoving your hand in the water and grabbing for it. You catch it by baiting a line and slowly drawing the fish into your lair, so to speak. Have the same approach toward tense situations.

7. *Do not think of defeat.* A great athlete, Tommy Hendricks, once wrote, "Whenever our team loses, I forget that and focus on the next game and make up my mind that the next game is going to be successful. I do that, not because I'm a poor loser, but because I'm so dreadfully afraid that if I keep my eyes on defeat, I will attract it to myself."

8. *Laugh it off.* Develop a sense of humor. Laugh at every little thing. Don't take yourself (and everything else) so seriously. Force yourself to laugh until it becomes a natural habit.

9. *Take time to reflect.* Frequently, think over your problems and be comforted that you are not alone. There is a Higher Being who has already gone through your adversities. He understands. "In the day of my trouble I sought the Lord," says the psalmist. (Psalm 77:2.) Talk your problem over with God. Tell Him just how you feel. Do so in a quiet spot in your home or house of worship. He will help you relax and melt your tense feelings.

DO NOT TREMBLE

Why should you lose self-control? You are a child of God, yet you will tell me that you cannot stop trembling when you are faced with certain situations. Does God tremble? If not, neither should you. Perhaps you have become separated from God and you are thinking weakness because you fear you cannot overcome the problem you face. The moment you think weakness, all the old fears start to attack you, and they make the most of it. Train yourself to *think strong* and your fears scurry away. Control your thoughts. If you let them run riot they will stir the subconscious and nervous system into erratic action and then you become "very nervous." You must manage your thoughts or they will control you.

YAWN AND RELAX

If your jaws, lips and neck muscles tighten, it's a warning symptom of impending stress. Try yawning. Open wide with a real big yawn. Wag your jaw a little bit. Chew on air with your mouth open. This exercise is used by vocal students to give them more flexible jaws and throat muscles. It helps relax them. It can do the same for you.

AVOID NOISE

Yes, noise is an irritant. In fact, even when you sleep, you can "hear" sounds entering your bedroom for they register on the mind and cause unnecessary mental activity. Avoid noise from the annoying ticking of a clock to a loud radio. Insulate your home. Heavy drapes, bookcases, rugs, upholstered furniture all tend to absorb noise from next door and in your own home. Get away from the city into the quiet country for recuperative and nerve-healing treatment.

Thomas Edison once said that city noises must inevitably grow greater and that the man of the future will be deaf. Noises are on the increase so insulate yourself against them. Improve your nutrition by means of a controlled fasting program of pure and natural foods. Develop mental strength. Help to noise-proof your home — and noise-proof yourself by strong will power.

To noise-proof your mind, close your eyes. Concentrate on them on the spot between your eyebrows and silently repeat to yourself the word "peace." Let your muscles slump down. *Let go. Let go. Let go. Let go. Let go.* Mentally *let go* of your face muscles, your neck muscles, chest, abdomen, back, legs, feet, arms, etc. Become a rag doll. *Peace. Peace. Peace. Peace. Peace.*

DEVELOP A POSITIVE ATTITUDE

So many of the ills that afflict mankind are the results of past suggestions to the subconscious mind, repeated so often that they have become subconscious habits of thought. Of course, we did not give these suggestions to the subconscious mind knowingly or intentionally, but the line of thought of those around us became impressed on it; or the subconscious mind was impressed by our manner of living, or our point of view sank into it deeply. Negative thoughts — envy, jealousy, fear, hatred, anger — all produce an unhealthy influence on the subconscious and nervous system. Develop a positive attitude — build thoughts of love, hope, faith, kindness. Build for good. Look up. Tell yourself that Divine Peace is in your mind, in your body, in your affairs. When you seek help from a Higher Source, when you open your thoughts to that Great Being, then help is given to you.

Certainly, to rebuild your health, you must first start with your mental attitude. Once you've attuned your thoughts to the Supreme Being, you're on the way to natural health through controlled fasting.

High Spots of Chapter 21:

1. We live in tense times, so learn to insulate yourself by proper diet and mental attitude.
2. Unnatural foods introduce chronic irritants and waste substances into the bloodstream which irritate delicate nerve endings.
3. Re-read the special controlled fasting plan that strengthened and cured nervous disorders.
4. Build the 9-step plan for melting tension, in your life.
5. Avoid noise. Reduce noise.
6. Develop a positive attitude.

22

How Controlled Fasting Can Be the Key to Your Entire Self-Renewal of Body and Mind

THE "MIRACLE" OF SELF-RENEWAL

The rewards for your valiant efforts to restore health by means of controlled fasting emphasize *self-renewal*. Your mind and your body will undergo regeneration, rejuvenation until you will feel that life *is* worth living because your life has become better than it was. By means of improved nutrition, corrective living habits, Nature has been able to renovate your insides and outsides until self-renewal has opened the door to good health. Following are important nutrition guidelines for your daily use.

NUTRITION GUIDELINE

To enjoy better health through controlled fasting, here is your guideline:

1. Serve as many foods in the original state as possible — fresh fruits and vegetables, nuts, certified whole milk, natural cheese and cold-pressed vegetable oils.
2. Eat a diet high in *protein*. Include:
   (a) Meat, including the variety meats — liver, kidney, brain, heart — poultry and sea food. Cook meat as little as possible because protein is injured by prolonged or high heat. Avoid pork.
   (b) Dairy products, eggs, unprocessed cheese and medically certified milk.
   (c) The legumes, soy and other beans.

3. Use *fruits* and *vegetables* (grown without the use of poisonous chemical sprays if possible). Cook vegetables with a minimum of water, at low heat, and for as short a time as possible. Use the liquid.
4. Use freshly ground WHOLE GRAIN CEREALS and FLOURS, for they contain more protein, all the B-complex vitamins, Vitamin E, minerals and unsaturated fatty acids.
5. Use cold-processed vegetable oils, which are an excellent source of essential unsaturated fatty acids.

AVOID THESE FOODS

1. *Avoid* the use of refined *sugar*. It provides no nutrients except carbohydrates. Excessive consumption is a prominent factor in dental decay and reduces the appetite for nourishing food. Honey may be used with discretion.

2. *Avoid* the use of *white flour*. It has had the vital elements of the grain removed, and enrichment replaces only a few of them. Frequently bleaching and preservative agents are added which may be harmful.

3. *Avoid* the use of such foods as bread, pastries, ice cream, cheese and cold meats which contain chemical additives. These are often used as preservatives, coloring and flavoring agents, emulsifiers, extenders, sweeteners, stabilizers, etc.

4. *Avoid* the use of poultry and meats produced with hormones to stimulate growth and to add weight.

5. *Avoid* the use of hydrogenated fats and oils. They contain mainly saturated fatty acids.

6. *Avoid* heated or processed milk, processed cheese foods and chocolate.

DON'T ABUSE YOURSELF

Whether on or off your controlled fasting program, do not abuse your body. It is unhealthy and unwise to overburden your system with a bulk of food. When a body gland or organ is overworked, it leads to a breakdown. Your body is like an automobile. It must be properly maintained, cared for and treated if it will serve you properly. Select foods carefully. Those that are organically grown are especially desired. Here, then, is a little guide for you to follow, not only for controlled fasting but for improved health.

BASIC HEALTH BUILDING STEPS

Here is a step-by-step plan to build your health as you self-renew yourself through controlled fasting. Even after you have recovered lost health, you need to continue to practice rightful living if you want to remain in good physical (and mental) shape.

1. *Variety is important.* Except when following a special internal cleansing diet, remember that variety in foods is important. There is no all-perfect food. Get enough vitamins, minerals, proteins, enzymes, etc., from a variety of fresh and organically grown fruits, vegetables, meats, fish, poultry, nuts, beans, etc.

2. *Fertile soil foods* are a "must." Insist upon them. Foods raised on poor soils are just as poor. If foods are raised with synthetic chemicals they will have residue picked up from those chemicals. Organically raised crops do not need sprays. If unable to obtain organically raised foods, then wash or scrub the fruits or vegetables as much as possible to get off as much as you can of the toxic wastes.

3. *Be cheerful.* A depressed mind produces a depressed body. Learn to look on the bright side of things. Relaxation follows with a cheerful attitude. Tension constricts arteries and veins leading to impaired circulation of blood and lymph, thereby hindering over-all body nourishment to cells and tissues and vital body organs.

4. *Breathe fresh air.* Regularly, get into a fresh air section of your town and breathe deeply — in and out — over and over again. This ventilates the deep extremities of your lungs.

5. *Exercise.* Brisk walking, swimming cycling, mild sports are all helpful. Do not over-exert yourself. When you exercise your body, you cause an alternate tensing and relaxing of muscles; this stimulates a rapid blood flow and speeds up the transportation of nutritive materials and excretion of wastes. There is self-renewal in movement! Don't let yourself stagnate.

6. *Bathe regularly* so you can wash your skin and cleanse off

sweat gland wastes. Pores should be kept open so waste materials can properly be excreted. A nightly bath should be part of your health plan. It's relaxing and you'll sleep better, too.

7. *Raw foods.* Eat as many raw foods as you can. Raw fruits and vegetables, raw nuts and seeds. Cooking and processing will destroy enzymes which your body needs to enable it to perform most vital activities. Enzymes are found solely in raw foods so eat many of these. A good tip is to begin most meals with a raw food such as salad greens or seasonable vegetables.

8. *Water is essential.* Water helps in food assimilation, transportation of nutrients to body tissues, and also elimination of toxic wastes. Water drinking (bottled spring water, if possible) should be part of your self-renewal plan. When fluid intake is adequate (at least 8 glasses daily or 2 quarts) there is less likelihood of constipation problems. Fluids are present in raw fruits and vegetables, too, and their extracted juices.

9. *Cook* with low heat, with as little water as possible. Cooked vegetable liquid may be rich in precious nutrients so use this for a sauce. Many vegetables have enough water for their own cooking. Try steaming vegetables.

10. *Meats cooked rare* retain more nutrients than if subjected to long cooking processes. Frying is undesirable because this method breaks up fat globules in the food which renders it less digestible. Frying also coats the food with a heavy insoluble fat. Best types of cookware are those made of stainless steel and glass. Shun aluminum vessels. Teflon-coated cookware is said to be safe up to 572° F.

11. *Vegetables* should not be peeled, for the most part, since the outer layers contain most of the nutritive elements. This applies to fruits, too. Edible skins and rinds should not be tossed away. When purchasing vegetables, select the greener and more colorful variety. Try to use the greener outer leaves of head vegetables, of celery tops, of most root vegetables.

12. *Spinach, chard* contains oxalic acid which will interfere with internal absorption of calcium and other minerals. It's best to shun these vegetables. Try kale, mustard greens, escarole.

13. *Sprouts* should be part of your health-renewal program. Alfalfa sprouts are especially recommended because they can sweep

your insides clean. Ask at any health store for sprouts.

14. *Read labels*. When purchasing any canned or packaged food, read the labels. Some foods are not legally required to list ingredients so be wary of them. Avoid foods that have been smoked or chemically preserved. Select sun-dried fruits instead of sulfur-dried foods. Your beef, poultry and fish should be obtained from outlets that do not deal with chemically fed animals.

15. *Fertile eggs*. These are higher in nutrient value. Infertile eggs may have longer storage life but do not have the "germ of life" which is so precious.

16. *Bread is the staff of life*. This is bread made from 100% whole grains. Avoid bleached flour which is inferior in health benefit. Stone ground flour possesses greater nutritional power because of a slow grinding process that uses less heat generation. Select breads made from whole millet, soy, oats, etc. Here's a tip — the fact that a label reads "wheat flour" does not mean it is pure. The label should say 100% Whole Wheat Flour.

17. *Fats and oils* should be cold-pressed and from a vegetable source.

18. *Canned fruits* may be used if the label reads that they are canned in their own juices. If canned in heavy or extra-heavy syrup, there is a high commercial sugar quantity.

19. *Enjoy life*. Yes, enjoy life. Get your recreation. Sleep well. Laugh often. Protect your mind and your body from harm. Shield yourself from abuse with wholesome inner dignity. Fortify your life by self-renewal of health by means of controlled fasting.

EPILOGUE

During a period of just 24 hours, this has been happening to your body. Your *heart* has beat 103,689 times. Your *blood* has travelled 168,000 miles. Your *lungs* have taken 23,040 breaths and have absorbed 438 cubic feet of air. Your *digestive system* has processed 2½ pounds of food and 2.9 quarts of liquid. Your *vocal chords* have spoken about 4,800 words. Getting through the chores of the day involves over 600 *muscles* and more than 7 million *brain* cells. These functions must continue in smooth progression, in smooth working order. This means that your body parts must be kept clean, well lubricated, youthful. Internal toxemia can undermine the machinery of your body with as much destructive power as rust or debris or dirt that gets into the working parts of any machine. Keep your insides clean. Improve health by means of *controlled fasting* and your whole life is bound to take a turn for the better in a great number of ways.

You are charged with the responsibility of taking care of the most wonderful "living machine" ever created: your body. Learn to take care of it.

We now stand at the crossroads. Together, we have gone along the journey, the quest for natural health that has controlled fasting as the keystone. As we pause before we part, there is just one note I must mention. It is a serious note. As you feel more youthful, as you enjoy greater vitality, as you look younger, you will see those you love the most continue to decay, to pass out of life long before their time. They did not take advantage of the great law of life — that of maintaining a healthy inside body. These same circumstances happened in my personal life and it sparked me to write this book, to tell others of my discoveries of controlled fasting so they, too, can partake of the Fountain of Youth this fasting can provide. Use this wisdom of the health techniques in this book carefully, and it will reward you well.

Books on Health, Nutrition

Vitamin E—Your Key to a Healthy Heart
Herbert Bailey

WHY IS VITAMIN E therapy for mankind's foremost killing disease still controversial in the United States? This is one of the questions asked and answered in this slashing, fully documented book. It tells how the efficacy of Vitamin E in the treatment of cardio-vascular disease was discovered by Dr. Evan Shute of Canada, and of the remarkable cures effected by him and his brother, also a doctor . . . how the author himself suffered a severe heart attack and how in a short time he was restored to normal, active life by massive doses of the vitamin . . . how a barrier against Vitamin E has been erected in this country by the medical traditionalists of the American Medical Association at the same time that it is being widely used with spectacular results in such medically advanced countries as England, Germany, France, Italy, and Russia . . . how continuing study indicates that Vitamin E may be an effective preventative for a variety of other diseases.

HERBERT BAILEY is a veteran medical reporter who has informed the American public about other epochal medical discoveries before they were accepted and used.

224 pages   **#1514 paper: $1.65**

THE SOYBEAN COOKBOOK   Dorothea Van Gundy Jones
Over 350 kitchen-tested recipes for using the versatile soybean in the family menu from salads and souffles to meat replacement main dishes and desserts. "An interesting and valuable book . . . delightful foods can be made quite rich in protein and very palatable as well."—**Health Culture.**
256 pages   #1770 paper: $1.45   #1805 cloth: $3.25

If your bookstore is out of stock on any of the above titles, you can order books directly from ARC BOOKS, Inc., 219 Park Avenue South, New York, N.Y. 10003. Enclose check or money order for list price of books plus 10¢ per book for postage and handling. No C.O.D.

Food Facts and Fallacies

The Intelligent Person's Guide to Nutrition and Health

Carlton Fredericks, Ph.D. and Herbert Bailey

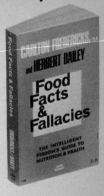

THIS IS a fascinating, excitingly readable book full of the essential facts that every modern thinking person should know about what he eats, what he should eat, and health. Dr. Carlton Fredericks, for the past 25 years one of our most eminent experts on nutrition has a devoted following which numbers in the millions. This informed group has had the benefit of his unbiased holistic approach to nutrition and his dedication to preventative medicine. They reject the cliche that "ignorance is bliss" or that it is "smart to be gullible." In what is probably the most comprehensive work in print on this subject for the layman, Dr. Fredericks (with his co-author Herbert Bailey) amplifies and clarifies many previously tested discoveries and much that only recently has found its way into medical and bio-chemical scientific research. Herbert Bailey, his co-author, is a pioneer whose many books and magazine articles have spearheaded recognition of medical discoveries which might otherwise be lost to public use. Never before has there appeared in a single volume for the general public so much real information, so complete a picture of the latest research on nutrition and health as will be found in **FOOD FACTS AND FALLACIES.**

380 pages   **#1726 paper: $1.95**

ARTHRITIS CAN BE CURED   Bernard Aschner, M.D.

If you are one of the millions of arthritis victims or if a friend or someone in your family suffers from an arthritic disease, this book can bring new hope into your life. Arthritis is officially considered to be an intractable and almost incurable malady. The most widely accepted treatments, at best, are long-term and slow to bring results; at worst, pointless or even harmful. However, despite the almost universally pessimistic attitude toward the disease, the author of this book, Dr. Bernard Aschner, maintains that arthritis really can be cured; painful, prolonged suffering can be eliminated; incapacitated persons can return to active, useful occupations. And he explains, in clear, easy-to-understand language for the layman, exactly how this may be done.

240 pages   **#1764 paper: $1.45**

TURN PAGE FOR ORDERING INFORMATION

Get Well Naturally

Linda Clark

LINDA CLARK believes that relieving human suffering and obtaining optimum health should be mankind's major goal. She insists that it does not matter whether a remedy is orthodox or unorthodox, currently praised or currently scorned in medical circles—as long as it works for you. Mrs. Clark, who is also the author of **Stay Young Longer,** makes a plea for the natural methods of treating disease —methods which do not rely on either drugs or surgery. Drawing not only from well-known sources but also from folklore and from the more revolutionary modern theories, she presents a wealth of information about diseases ranging from alcoholism to ulcers. Here are frank discussions of such controversial modes of treatment as herbal medicine, auto-therapy, homeopathy, and human electronics, plus some startling facts and theories about nutrition and about the natural ways of treating twenty-two of the most serious illnesses that plague modern man.

410 pages   **#1762 paper: $1.65**

INTERNATIONAL VEGETARIAN COOKERY   Sonya Richmond

This book proves that vegetarian cookery, far from being dull and difficult to prepare, can open up completely new and delightful vistas of haute cuisine. Miss Richmond, who has traveled throughout the world, has arranged the book alphabetically according to countries, starting with Austria and going through to the United States. She gives recipes for each country's most characteristic vegetarian dishes and lists that country's outstanding cheeses.

192 pages   #1510 cloth: $3.75
                    #1483 paper: $1.75

THE BOOK OF SALADS   Hyla Nelson O'Connor

Here are over two hundred recipes for gourmet salads that are both healthful and delicious. The author also gives valuable information on selecting and handling salad greens and includes thirteen recipes for basic, nutritious salad dressings with many variations.

144 pages   #374 cloth: $3.50

How to be Healthy With Natural Foods

Edward E. Marsh

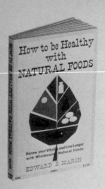

Do you feel sluggish, tired, old beyond your years? Do you get frequent colds, lack pep and energy, feel overweight and stuffed? Chances are that you are not eating the right foods. The average American's diet today consists of innutritious processed foods, fats and starches, insufficient vitamins and minerals—a diet that contains little or nothing of value and, usually, much that is downright harmful. **HOW TO BE HEALTHY WITH NATURAL FOODS** shows that it is possible to maintain optimum health and eliminate colds and other chronic ailments by using only wholesome, natural foods and by eliminating from your diet foods that are harmful or that contain nothing of value to your body. In this concise, practical book on nutrition, the author presents simple, tried and tested rules for the selection of healthful and tasty foods, including suggestions for specific diets to build and maintain vitality, protect against senility, and promote vigorous health and long life.

160 pages

#1691 cloth: $3.25
#1620 paper: $1.45

HOW TO BE HEALTHY WITH YOGA
Sonya Richmond

How to improve your health without the aid of drugs, by practicing the ancient art of yoga. All exercises are accompanied by explanatory illustrations, and a valuable chapter deals with what foods to eat and how to eat them. This book is clearly written and gives vital information, not only on being healthy but also on relaxing and coping with problems. Separate chapters cover tension, emotional stress, insomnia and fatigue, indigestion, backache, bad posture, asthma, bronchitis, arthritis, and other common maladies; and each chapter tells how yoga can help you overcome these problems.

160 pages

#1002 cloth: $2.50
#1004 paper: $ .95

90 DAYS TO A BETTER HEART
John X. Loughran

The commonsense way to a healthier heart and longer life within 90 days through the use of natural, unrefined foods and a program of graduated exercise. The author, a long-time crusader for better nutrition, stresses the important role of vitamins in controlling fatigue and tension and sheds considerable light on the mystery of cholesterol.

208 pages

#1793 paper: $1.45

HEALTH, FITNESS, and MEDICINE BOOKS

1764 **Arthritis Can be Cured,** Aschner, M.D. (1.45)

2128 **The Doctor Who Looked at Hands,** Ellis (1.45)

1726 **Food Facts and Fallacies,** Fredericks & Bailey (1.95)

1762 **Get Well Naturally,** Linda Clark (1.65)

1083 **Health Foods and Herbs,** Hunter (.95)

1902 **Healthy Hair,** Thompson & Thompson (1.45)

1135 **Heart Disease and High Blood Pressure,** Hutchin, M.D. (1.45)

2131 **Helping Your Health with Enzymes,** Wade (1.95)

1620 **How to be Healthy With Natural Foods,** Marsh (1.45)

2133 **The Jack LaLanne Way to Vibrant Good Health** (1.65)

2134 **The Low-Fat Way to Health and Longer Life,** Morrison (1.65)

2135 **Magic Minerals,** Wade (1.95)

2132 **The Natural Way to Health Through Controlled Fasting,** Wade, (1.95)

1793 **90 Days to a Better Heart,** Loughran (1.45)

1831 **Open Door to Health,** Miller (1.45)

1792 **The Pulse Test,** Coca, M.D. (1.45)

1771 **Rebuilding Health,** Waerland (1.45)

1137 **Slipped Discs,** Hutchin, M.D. (.95)

1157 **Stomach Ulcers,** Hutchin, M.D. (.95)

1514 **Vitamin E: Your Key to a Healthy Heart,** Bailey

1147 **The Whole Truth About Allergy,** Hirschfeld, M.D. (.95)

1221 **Your Allergic Child,** Hirschfeld, M.D. (1.45)

1483 **International Vegetarian Cookery,** Richmond (1.75)

1770 **The Soybean Cookbook,** Lager & Jones (1.45)

1439 **Mushroom Recipes,** Countess Murphy (1.45)

1740 **June Roth's Thousand Calorie Cook Book,** Roth (3.50)

1004 **How to be Healthy with Yoga,** Richmond (.95)

2135 **Jack LaLanne's Foods for Glamour** (1.65)

1656 **Yoga for Beauty,** Volin & Phelan (.95)

If your bookstore is out of stock on any of the above titles, you can order books directly from ARC BOOKS, Inc., 219 Park Avenue South, New York, N.Y. 10003. Enclose check or money order for list price of books plus 10¢ per book for postage and handling. No C.O.D.